EBORACENSIS
Comitatus (cuius locales olim
Brigantes appellabantur) Lon-
gitudinis Latitudinis hominibus
numero reliquis illustrior
An°. Dñi 1577

OCEANVS

Blakay more

THE

Pickering

The foreft of pickering

THE

KILNAM

EST

Yorkes worth

RIDING

WIGHTON

BEVERLEY

HULL

Humber

BARTON

Marthe lande
Diche marthe

BURTON

Axholme
Inful

LINCOL:

NOTTIN

GAMIÆ

PARS

NIÆ PARS

Scala Milliarum 9.

Augustinus Rycher, Anglus Sculpsit An° Dñi 1577

GOODBYE TO YORKSHIRE

GOODBYE TO YORKSHIRE

by

ROY HATTERSLEY

LONDON
VICTOR GOLLANCZ LTD
1976

ISBN 0 575 02201 9

The lines from W. H. Auden's *In Praise of Limestone* are from *Collected Shorter Poems 1927–1957*, © W. H. Auden, 1966, and are reprinted by permission of Faber & Faber Ltd and Random House Inc.

Printed in Great Britain by
The Camelot Press Ltd, Southampton

For my mother

CONTENTS

ILLUSTRATIONS

Endpaper map: Saxton's Map of Yorkshire, 1577 (*courtesy Trustees of the British Museum*)

Following page 64

"Goodbye to Yorkshire": Sheffield, Abbeydale File Works (*courtesy Sheffield Telegraph*)

"Wish You Were Here": Bridlington Sands and Bridlington Harbour (*courtesy Yorkshire Post*)

"They Also Serve": the Sheffield blitz, 1940 (*courtesy Sheffield Telegraph*)

"The Name on the Knife Blade": Sheffield Panorama (*courtesy City of Sheffield*

"Limestone Country": Pen-y-Ghent and Malham Cove (*courtesy Yorkshire Post*)

"Out of Season": the Winter Gardens at Scarborough (*courtesy Scarborough Council*)

"Heart and Homeland": the Wharfe near Bolton Abbey (*photo Oliver Hatch*)

"The Halfway Place": Knaresborough (*photo Peter Baker*)

Following page 128

"Church Triumphant": York Minster (*courtesy Dean and Chapter of York Minster*)

"Work and Worship": Fountains Abbey (*courtesy Yorkshire Post*)

"Skylark's Song": Haworth Parsonage (*courtesy Bradford Telegraph and Argus*)

"Get Stuck In!": Sheffield Wednesday Football Club, 1935 (*courtesy Sheffield Wednesday Football Club, photo Photopress*)

"Before the Fall": Yorkshire County Cricket Club, 1923 (*courtesy Sheffield Telegraph*)

"Hard and Proud": miners at the Orgreave Colliery, South Yorkshire (*courtesy Sheffield Telegraph*)

"Likely Lad": heavy forging in Sheffield (*courtesy Firth Brown Ltd, photo River Don Stampings Ltd*)

"The Infant Gentleman": the transporter bridge, Middlesbrough (*courtesy County of Cleveland and Priest Furnaces Ltd*), a rolling mill (*courtesy British Steel Corporation*)

"No Mean City": Leeds Town Hall (*courtesy Leeds City Council*)

"Glad Tidings to Zion": Huddersfield Railway Station (*courtesy Kirklees Metropolitan Council*)

"Builded Here": Hyde Park, Sheffield (*photo Castle Photos, courtesy City of Sheffield*)

ACKNOWLEDGEMENTS

Goodbye to Yorkshire was begun a few weeks before the General Election of February 1974. During the two years which followed, it dominated all my holidays and occupied those small parts of my weekends left free by the Foreign Office and the Sparkbrook Constituency. I am deeply grateful for the understanding of my neglected family and friends.

Writing these twenty-two essays gave me greater sustained pleasure than anything else I have ever done, not least because it encouraged me to read what others have written about Yorkshire during the last two hundred years. Most of the quotations are specifically acknowledged in the text. But my thanks are particularly due to Faber & Faber and Random House Inc. for the permission to quote the opening and closing lines of W. H. Auden's *In Praise of Limestone*, to Faber & Faber for lines from Philip Larkin's *Whitsun Weddings*, to Secker & Warburg and Mrs Sonia Brownwell Orwell for a passage from George Orwell's *The Road to Wigan Pier*, to William Heinemann Ltd and A. D. Peters & Co Ltd for a passage from J. B. Priestley's *The Good Companions*, and to Mr Henry Pelling for his description of the Bradford Conference of the Independent Labour Party and to Professor Asa Briggs for his account (in *Victorian Cities*) of the building of Leeds Town Hall and the creation of industrial Middlesbrough.

The Town Clerks (now often called Chief Executives) of Hull, Leeds, Scarborough and Huddersfield (now called Kirklees) provided invaluable information about Yorkshire local government and local history. Mr Leslie Hodge (sometime Senior Geography Master of the Sheffield City Grammar School) was kind enough to read and comment upon the essay which describes "Limestone Country". Mr J. G. Fearnley, Choir Secretary, generously arranged for me to be present during a rehearsal of the Huddersfield Choral Society's 1975 Carol Concert. Harry Parker (Photograph Manager of the Sheffield *Telegraph and Star*) provided pictures of Yorkshire and introduced me to colleagues on other papers who were kind enough to do the same. Photographs are acknowledged individually in the List of Illustrations.

Great as is my debt to all those who helped in the creation of *Goodbye to Yorkshire*, my deepest thanks are due to the county itself, the hero as well as the scene and subject of these essays and the only true begetter of this humble tribute.

R. H.

ONE

Goodbye to Yorkshire

———————————

GOODBYE TO YORKSHIRE

Yorkshire is an idea not a place. Of course it is not solely the creation of fey literary imagination. Yorkshire has nothing in common with Camelot. For one thing, no self-respecting Yorkshireman would throw away a perfectly good sword. For another it was fact before it turned into fantasy. Once upon a time—before the Redcliffe Maud Report, the Boundary Commission and the Local Government Act—Yorkshire was marked on the real maps of the real world, an English county only divided into three Ridings because it was too big to be governed in single splendour. But even then, before it only formally and factually existed as the name of a cricket team, the noun Yorkshire was more spiritual than geographical.

Yorkshire represented a set of particular values—the compulsive desire to compete and the obsessive need to win, a certainty in the righteousness of every favoured cause and truculent scepticism about other people's convictions, an absolute faith in the eventual triumph of industry and the ultimate victory of thrift, the unrestrained aggression that gets men knocked down and the determined pride that makes them stand up again, the belief in the importance of self-improvement and the propriety of self-confidence, a weakness for mock piety and false sentiment and—above all else—a strong suspicion that the tender virtues are not really virtues at all.

The attributes for which Yorkshire and Yorkshiremen will be remembered were essentially the product of Victorian England. They are not the qualities for which Yorkshire has always stood. For a thousand years it stood for nothing in particular. Before the enclosures Yorkshire was hardly different from the ordinary counties. The characteristics which made it more proverbial than provincial only began to stir with the industrial revolution and the coming of the muck that goes with the brass and the sweat that changes one into the other.

Until the nineteenth century there were no immutable economic laws which united Barnsley, Bridlington and Boroughbridge and yet somehow distinguished them from what lay east of the Pennines and south of the Humber. Before the Napoleonic Wars there was no common cultural heritage or spiritual yearning that embraced Hull, Haworth and

Halifax. Yorkshire started to stand for something when all that was hard, heavy and arduous in Victorian England began to flourish in the county—coal cut from deep seams, blooms and billets of hot steel manhandled under massive steam hammers, wool spun and woven not at home but during long days spent in the company's cold sheds. To survive any or all of that, the families that lived in the lath and plaster back-to-back houses had to espouse the oppressive virtues and the stern values. It was not a time in which the tender could survive. In parts of Yorkshire—the farms high up on the millstone grit, the ports whose fishermen spent six months each year on the North Sea—times had always been hard. By the time Queen Victoria came to the throne, "hard" was the word that characterised life in two-thirds of the county. The plant that took root in that cold and stony ground had flowers as well as thorns.

Within the dark satanic mills and the little houses that huddled round them there developed a determination to begin building the New Jerusalem. Some saw it as their spiritual obligation. Others thought it their political duty. Often the strands of belief intertwined. At the beginning of the nineteenth century Ebenezer Elliot's south Yorkshire poetry was as religious as it was revolutionary—"When wilt thou save the people O God of Mercy, when? The people, Lord, the people. Not crowns and thrones but men." At the century's end, the Independent Labour Party was founded in Bradford and brought into British politics that revivalist fervour and rollicking music that made Sundays joyous in the doric temples and gothic tabernacles which had been built all over Yorkshire by the Methodists (Primitive and Reform), Wesleyans, Unitarians, Baptists and Congregationalists.

But since Yorkshiremen are sceptical as well as cautious there was always a predisposition to hedge their bets on the Socialist Millennium and Second Coming with small investments in brightness and beauty here and now. So they turned to brass bands and chrysanthemum clubs (both of which were cheap as well as cheerful) or enrolled in choral societies, where they could praise God, enjoy themselves and learn to read music, all for a single subscription. Those who preferred a more formal sort of self-improvement went to the Mechanics Institute and carried home a weekly book-box full of Sunday reading. Others spent the Sabbath moments between chapel and chapel walking in the local arboretum or botanical gardens where, the trees and flowers being labelled with Latin names and countries of origin, there was a big enough element of learning to justify the pleasure. Pleasure alone was not enough. There had to be the prospect of gaining something—education, advancement or salvation.

The pursuit of those aims was never rash or reckless. Risks were certainly taken. Yorkshiremen risked their money by sinking mine shafts and risked their backs by actually cutting the coal. Without risks, the railway kings would never have been crowned. In Hull and York, Quaker risks were taken with the fruits of Quaker thrift. As a result, the family firms were turned into mustard, chocolate and soap empires. In Sheffield, with each innovation in the production of steel or the perfection of cutlery there were men willing to risk the money they had made working in the old ways on the calculation that they would make a fortune out of the new. But the wager was never casually laid. The risks were always reduced to the point where it was difficult to distinguish between gamble and investment. For Yorkshire was careful country.

Indeed, "careful" is one of the great Yorkshire euphemisms, a word that conjures up all the mystery of the tea-caddy on the Wakefield mantelpiece and all the magic of the ten-shilling note inside it. Once it was just one tiny part of the county's indicative vocabulary which contained an exclusive Yorkshire response to every situation.

History, for instance, does not record how, in the summer of 1642, John Hotham responded to the Duke of York's demand that the gates of Hull be opened and Charles Stuart's army admitted to the City and Port. But there can be no doubt the proper Yorkshire reply to the suggestion that due fealty be shown to the King who ruled by Divine Right. "Tha' what?" Despite its question mark, "tha' what?" is not a request for information, but a statement of incredulity. It is an admission of neither deafness nor inattention. "Tha' what?" loses much in translation but an English version, of sorts, can be constructed. It reads "Whilst I heard what you said, the opinions you advanced are so bizarre that I will only believe that you seriously hold those views if you repeat them, word for word." All of which represents the right Yorkshire reaction to an invitation to join the side which could not win the Civil War and pay ship money for the privilege.

"Tha' what?" is the proper response to the suggestion that Yorkshiremen are either "mardy" or "nesh". "Nesh" is both an adjective and a verb. Footballers who are not prepared to risk a broken leg in every tackle are accused of "neshing" it. Young men watching from the terraces who protect themselves from cold with scarves and gloves are "nesh". "Mardy" is a related condition—a childish petulance, a tendency to whine about trivial inconvenience, the propensity to complain about slight hurt or superficial injury. The spirit of Yorkshire was born during an age when such weaknesses were openly despised and publicly reviled. George

Hudson could not have built his railway from York to London and lied his way into Parliament and society if he had been nesh—or if the men who dug the cuttings and laid the rails had been mardy.

The spirit which reviled the mardy, despised the nesh and replied "tha' what?" to every suggestion of giving up or falling down could not survive the coming of the welfare state. But it was not only the arrival of compassion that destroyed the Yorkshire ethos. The hard industries which made Victorian Yorkshire prosperous slipped into decline and the virtues and vices which made employment in them tolerable no longer seemed necessary. As coal and shipping turned into last century's assets and as Yorkshiremen learned to rely on Factory Acts and Road Safety Committees rather than self-protection, the idea of Yorkshire began to disappear with the society that created it. Of course, much that was hard old Yorkshire is better gone and best forgotten. The nineteenth-century obsession with success glorified the victors without a moment's thought for the vanquished over whom they climbed. The folk tales are told about the few who climbed from rags to riches rather than the many who remained in ragged misery all their lives. But there was much that was good—and a little that was splendid—about old Yorkshire that deserves at least a decent burial and a respectable ham tea to send it on its way.

Included amongst the honourable dead is the idea of "quality"— quality used as an adjective to praise a suit or a knife. Quality suits are made of worsted, one hundred per cent pure new wool. They are usually navy blue and often double-breasted. They are the product of careful saving and expert craftsmanship. They have to last for a decade and, in consequence, are only worn on Sundays. A quality knife says "made in Sheffield" on the blade. It was forged and ground by hand in a "little mester's" factory and was polished by a "buffer girl" with brown paper tied round her legs to protect them from the flying dust and grease. Obtaining quality knives and suits required arduous saving. Making them involved long hours of underpaid work. They could not survive the coming of cheap man-made fibres and cutlery machined smooth from blanks made in Hong Kong. When the world was made easier, Yorkshire shrank a little and stopped baking its own bread and making its own cakes and pastry. It turned instead to things in frozen packets and tin-foil called "convenience foods". In old Yorkshire it was different. The choice between quality and convenience was no choice at all.

Quality was not the only casualty of time. Inflation, football pools and hire purchase drove thrift out of fashion. Brass cornets and french horns which are cheap to buy, tedious to polish and difficult to master) have little appeal to a generation of young men who can afford electric guitars which can be played by anyone capable of plugging them in to a socket. Universal education overtook and undermined the need for the Mechanics Institute and the enthusiasm for the WEA. One by one, each condition and every circumstance that made Yorkshire a moral and spiritual force in Victorian England disappeared. What it once stood for lived on as a legend between the wars. Then even the legend began to look out of date.

Even Yorkshire's size—its last realistic claim to pride of place amongst the English counties—became unimportant. Before the 1950s (the years when local loyalty had at least a residual importance, and most men who played first-class cricket were born in the county whose badge they wore) Yorkshire could dominate the Championship. The County Cricket Club had two priceless assets—the will to win and a larger population from which to choose its team than any of its rivals. When other counties began to pick their bowlers from Brisbane and Barbados and their batsmen from Durban and Delhi one of those advantages vanished. The habit of winning vanished as well—and with it the will.

Of course, true to its traditions, old Yorkshire died hard. Indeed often it refused to believe that it had died at all. In 1958, when the County finished lower in the Championship table than at any other time in its history, Sir William Worsley (the President of the Club) was not prepared to admit that the world had changed. "Welcome," he cried at despondent County Members. "Welcome to the Annual Meeting of the Champion County. For we in Yorkshire know which is the Champion County, irrespective of what side happens to be at the top of the table at any one time." But despite such robust defences of the old values during the 1950s, the battle was lost.

Two decades later, even the formal boundaries were destroyed. Now, thanks to the reorganisation of local government, little boys in Hull must try to develop a passionate loyalty to "Humberside" and the County's regiments must lay up their colours in churches which stand not in county towns but in "various parts" of Metropolitan Districts. But the Parliamentary formality was hardly important—the last rites for a very dear departed. By the time Yorkshire was removed from the map, what it stood for only lived on in men's minds and memories—an image to inspire sons to greater efforts, and warn daughters to beware of men who still, at least spiritually, scrub their backs in old zinc baths in front of the kitchen fire and carefully count the housekeeping money.

The reality was long since dead. There are no politicians like John

Arthur Roebuck (who had "hardiness beyond all other mortals") to bring down governments almost single-handed by "placing unbounded confidence in himself and troubling his mind about very little else". "The way along from Leeds to Sheffield" is no longer "coal and iron, iron and steel" as it was when William Cobbett rode it. It is now a straight blank motorway that by-passes Chapeltown and Newmillersdam —a motorway like any other motorway, a road that leads to anywhere and from anywhere. Time and progress have ensured that the "iron forges" that Cobbett saw no longer illuminate the route "in the horrible splendour of their everlasting blaze". The horror is no longer necessary and the splendour (which it in part produced) has passed with it into history.

TWO

A South Yorkshire Boyhood

THE NAME ON THE KNIFE BLADE

ON THE DAY that I was born my grandmother wept to think that she should have a grandchild who would never see a green field. An invalid, she had travelled to Sheffield in a closed car, and all she knew of the city was a walk made thirty years before from the Victoria Station, through the Pond Street slums to the Edwardian shops along the Moor.

The Pond Street slums were demolished in 1930 during one of the earliest and most imaginative clearance programmes in English history. The Moor and its Edwardian shops were flattened by a ruder hand during two nights in December 1940. The Victoria Station still stands, but it is silent. No trains have pulled alongside its platforms since 1968. But one thing about Sheffield never changes. It is still the unknown city, the name on the knife blade and no more. That was true when Cobbett rode past in 1830. It is true today, now that the city boundaries have changed and half its municipal decisions are taken in Barnsley. Most of Britain knows as little about Sheffield as my grandmother did in 1932.

History is to blame. It set Sheffield at the foot of the Pennines on the millstone grit that made its grindstones and near to the water that drove them. Coal confirmed its place at the heart of nineteenth-century England but made it an industrial city where people work, not a commercial city which people visit. Until the early sixties, Sheffield had fewer hotels than most towns half its size and hardly any of the goodwill that replete salesmen and satisfied sales representatives carry home from Birmingham and Manchester.

But that is not the only reason why there is no sharp picture of Sheffield etched on the national mind. Sheffield has eight rivers and a thousand hills and although they are no longer the tools and the power of the city's trade they still have—as they have always had—an abiding influence on the character of the place. Sheffield is divided by them into suburbs as distinct and separate as the cutlery processes in which they each once specialised. The people of Walkley and Woodseats, Brightside and Broomhill still talk of "going into Sheffield" as if their excursion would take them to a friendly but distant place. Sheffield is less a unified city than a federation of sovereign suburbs which owe guarded allegiance to the Mayor and Corporation. Even before the arrival of the new Metropolitan

Borough, Sheffield extended its boundaries every ten years or so. When Dore in the south and Wadsley in the north first became part of the city they were never thought of as newcomers. They were just extra provinces added on to a loosely organised empire.

But the men of Woodseats and the women of Walkley have a devoted loyalty to the empire of which they are part and a passionate pride in its history. The history of Sheffield is largely the history of steel.

Huntsman invented the crucible process for making steel in Sheffield and every one of the city's schoolboys knows it. They may not know that King Eadred of Northumbria surrendered in their city's southern suburb and that, in consequence, England was united under a single monarch for the first time—even though the victorious King Ecgbert had given his name to a comprehensive school. But they know one fact about the *Canterbury Tales*—the Reeve carried a *thwittel* made in Sheffield. The tower where Mary Queen of Scots was imprisoned is left slowly crumbling and largely decayed; but the remains of an industrial revolution village are preserved and restored to their hard nineteenth-century efficiency. Its water-wheel turns. Its tilt hammer strikes. And twice a year steel—the stuff that made Sheffield famous—is once more fashioned into swords and plough-shares.

It is almost twenty years since the last tilt hammer pounded anvil in Sheffield and over twice as long since one of the city's football clubs won either Cup or League. Although the city has no time for any other winter game (Rugby League is unknown and Rugby Union has a precarious toe-hold on the southern boundary) only grandfathers can remember the last time a local team was carried through a cheering crowd on a beribboned bus with a trophy on the top deck. Supporters of Wednesday and United eye each other warily across the city lest by some freak of chance (merit being out of the question) the "other side" is first amongst the honours. The rivalry between the city's teams is of the fratricidal not fraternal variety. As a boy, I genuinely believed in the man who never ate bacon because its red and white stripes reminded him of Sheffield United—indeed in my blue-and-white Wednesday heart I applauded and supported his loyalty.

In winter I hated and despised Bramall Lane, but in summer—when it was transformed from the Hades of Sheffield United to the Elysium of the Yorkshire County Cricket Club—it was the only place I wanted to be. When Worcester beat Yorkshire for the first time in the history of the Championship I suffered every ball that was bowled. On the second and third days I arrived at the ground at half past eight—approximately the time I should have got to school—and took up my position on the balcony of the Victorian pavilion. Past St Mary's Church and the brewery chimneys, which were supposed to belch out particularly black smoke on days when Lancashire were batting in bad light, the city of Sheffield spread out up its hills and down its valleys. For the first time, I realised how green a city Sheffield was, with patches of park and long lines of trees running down from the suburbs to the city centre. The Bramall Lane pavilion has gone and the skyline of Sheffield is broken by a thousand tall new buildings. But the trees are still there, picked out against the hills which make Sheffield what it is.

A quarter of a century ago, Bramall Lane seemed to me the only flat cricket ground in Sheffield. I played my youthful strokes on wickets cut into hillsides where uppish shots to leg hit the ground a yard above the batsman's head and offside fielders waited for catches with eyes level to the batsman's boots. Gradients like that broke fielders' hearts but they made the reputation of municipal architects. Most of the virgin land available for housing after the war had been rejected twenty years earlier as too steep for practical building. Yet houses have been cut into, hung from and stuck on to the steep slopes of Gleadless, Woodside, Stannington and Netherthorpe. The maisonettes and the town houses, the point blocks and the flats have extended and elaborated the city skyline and provided a thousand new vantage points from which the city can be seen spreading out from the factory roofs of the East End, to Broomhill (John Betjeman's favourite English suburb) in the west.

Once the landmarks of Sheffield were monuments to piety and civic virtue: the "new" Town Hall built in the neo-gothic style in 1878; the Calver Street Chapel, designed two years later, to look like the Parthenon; the City Hall constructed in 1938 with massive ionic pillars, not to support the roof but to demonstrate the continuing belief that antiquity (even mock antiquity) is essential to power and glory. Now the philosophy has changed. There is nothing contrived or consciously decorative about Park Hill or Hyde Park flats. The estate at Woodside has reminded some people of a Tuscan hill village—but they were southern romantics. The style is subsumed in the intention that Sheffield's new buildings are good places to live and work in. They look confident that their intention is fulfilled and, therefore, right for the men and women of a confident city.

Men who spend their lives working with hot and sharp metal develop special virtues. Twenty years of bending and breaking steel will convince any man that no task is beyond him, given the tools and given the time. It will convince him too that caution as a virtue is second only to courage.

When a bloom or a billet goes back from the hammer to the furnace and a man carefully wipes his face with his sweat rag and carefully spits on the ingot as it passes, no contempt is intended. It is an admission that it still possesses hard hot strength, an indication that, even though he will shape it in the end, if he approaches it too rashly now its value and his bonus (and possibly a hand or eye) will vanish as quickly as his spittle sizzles away.

So Sheffield men are both cocky and cautious. They are sceptical too. They are particularly sceptical about the proposition that outside Sheffield there are places with ideas or habits or neighbours as good as theirs. Because of that, they have preserved pieces of the nineteenth century unspoilt by improvement. The Whitsuntide processions with their Sunday School choirs and captains who sing in public parks, the Star Walk for amateur athletes, the fishing competitions and the cycling clubs, like the pipeclayed steps and window-sills (some of them fifteen storeys in the sky), are part of an earlier, less sophisticated age. Sheffield kept its tram cars longer than any other English city. It kept them for good practical reasons and parted from them with solemn and formal regret. The "Last Tram" drove ceremoniously to the Town Hall to the tune of "Auld Lang Syne", and in the square where the unemployed rioted in 1926, the assembled Corporation bade it a sad last farewell.

Since the war Sheffield has said goodbye to half its past. Most of the "little mesters" have gone, and with their passing half of the historic trades have slipped into history. The craftsmanship of the cutlers is fighting a losing battle against the techniques of foreign mass-production. Even the rollers, turners and coggers increasingly employ brains and machinery for tasks which their fathers performed with muscle and sweat. But the traditional values abide. Sheffielders believe that all they need can be found by the banks of the Sheaf, the Don and the Porter. Oscar Wilde believed that "when good Americans die, they go to Paris". There is no doubt where good Sheffielders go. They go to Sheffield.

THEY ALSO SERVE

ON THE FIRST night they were turned back over the east coast—or, at least, so we were told the next morning. In fact, they never even set out. But at home in Sheffield, on the first full day of the war, we alternately glowed with pride and sighed with relief to think that the might of the Luftwaffe had been defeated all along a salient that stretched from Filey to Cleethorpes.

That first siren was the opening shot in the phoney war; but it seemed real enough at the time. For that moment the strips of brown paper had been stuck to the windows and the gas lamps turned down. It was to meet the challenge of that hour that we endured the distribution of fire-fighting equipment.

Airedale Road had received its quotas of ladders, axes and stirrup-pumps some weeks before Mr Neville Chamberlain's doleful announcement. Everybody knew that war would never really come, so the haggling went on with a clear Yorkshire conscience. We were a community of new owner-occupiers; struggling to keep mortgage payments up to date, rate demands met and bricks and mortar in good repair. Proprietary enthusiasm and financial necessity made Airedale Road a street of amateur odd-job men. Competition for the custody of ladders and stirrup-pumps was fierce and unscrupulous.

It was not the sort of contest that my father could win or would enter. We were at the end of the equipment queue and, in consequence, were allocated South Yorkshire's answer to the incendiary bomb. It consisted of a twelve-foot wooden pole topped with a device which might have been a small Victorian coal scuttle or a large Prussian steel helmet. The theory was simple. The fire-fighter enticed the flaming bomb into the metal scoop and then carried or lobbed it to safety. The practice was riddled with complication. For one thing any self-respecting incendiary bomb would have burned the scoop from the pole in a matter of seconds. For another, its inventor (a neighbour who never gave a clear answer about the royalties on his patent) was woefully unfamiliar with the work of Isaac Newton. The pole was so long and the scoop so heavy that it could only be manipulated by a fire-fighter sufficiently self-sacrificial to hold it so near to the business end that his arms would burn away with the pole.

At first we let it lie useless in the hall. Then it stood impotent and self-conscious against the outside wall. We ruminated on it for hours and tried to think of modifications. Was there not, my father asked (searching vainly for inspiration), an ancient army whose defeat resulted from the adoption of spears too long to handle. None of his fellow fire-fighters knew the answer. Ancient armies were irrelevant to the problems of civil defence equipment. They had no brickwork to point, slates to replace or guttering to keep free of leaves.

But all that was going on during the summer when the sirens sounded pre-arranged practice alarms, and the barrage-balloons went up in the middle of each morning and ended their morale-boosting day at tea-time every afternoon. The alert on the first night was, as far as we knew, the real thing. Duty was a concept that my infant mind did not fully understand. But I knew, with certainty, that whatever it was, we all had to do it now.

I soon learned that for people like us, duty meant fire-watching. Ours was a militantly patriotic road, inhabited by young steel works clerks and junior managers whose belligerence was uninhibited by their employment in reserved occupations. The business of defending their own road obsessed them. Careful rotas (thirty years after, I can associate the word with no other activity than fire-watching) were prepared at the beginning of each week and revised, indeed refined, every day. The nights were divided into two-hour stints and two able-bodied men were allocated to each watch.

For months my father's companion was missing. He neither responded to friendly words nor replied to formal letters. When his wife was spoken to, the result was immediate. Next night she appeared in his place and paced the black-out side by side with my father. The anger mounted and was compounded by embarrassment. It was decided that something must be done.

The patriotic young men decided to give him one last chance, followed by summary justice. If he did not make a cringing apology and give impeccable assurances about his future conduct, they would hit him. They assembled at his gate, unsure who would ask the first question or strike the first blow. I crouched at the front window to witness the first lynching ever to take place in a Sheffield suburb.

The errant fire-watcher appeared, resplendent in ginger harris-tweed plus fours, and approached his would-be tormentors. "You have," he said in deep reproach, "forced me to say things better left unsaid." The episode was not going in the way that any of us had hoped—any of us, that is, except the miserable absentee. Before the forces of righteousness could regain their moral balance he waved a lofty hand in the direction of his garage—the pre-fabricated asbestos kind that were advertised in Sunday papers on easy payment schemes.

"No doubt," he said, "you imagine that to be merely the place in which I keep my car." I certainly did. Indeed I had seen the Morris Opal through the dirty windows when I had gone in between the hedges to get my tennis ball. "It is more than that. When the siren sounds it is my duty to be in there working the machinery. I shall say no more." The young men mumbled an apology. I sank below the window-sill, limp with disappointment. For the next two years my father fire-watched alone.

They were two busy years for fire-watchers. Most nights there was a raid of sorts—a false alarm, a single incendiary bomb in a neighbour's garden, anti-aircraft shrapnel to collect and keep as prospective souvenirs. But some raids were special. The Sheffield blitz did not take us by surprise. Coventry had been hit in early December and the eight o'clock news had played the Coventry Carol after telling us that the cathedral was bombed and burning. It could only be a matter of time before the Luftwaffe moved its blitzkrieg north to the industrial cities of Yorkshire. Our chosen days were Thursday and Sunday the 12th and 15th of December. The factories escaped but the city centre was flattened—according to the gossip-mongers that the Ministry of Information posters warned us against, because an idiot in the Town Hall turned on the street lights by mistake.

On the first night we simply sat on the living-room floor and waited for it to be over. My grandmother, an invalid incapable of taking refuge in a real shelter, was protected by an invention created (but neither patented nor perfected) by the City Engineer's Department. The joists of the bedroom floor above her head were reinforced by steel girders that ran along the living-room ceiling. The girders were held in place by four steel columns, buried like tent poles in the foundations of our new, hard-earned, owned and occupied, semi-detached. My mother cried a little when they chipped away the plaster to take the ends of the girders and I fell into the hole cut in the floor-boards to let the tent poles through. In theory, if the house collapsed, the room in which we huddled with my grandmother would remain intact under the rubble. On the night of the first blitz we almost believed it.

The Luftwaffe came in waves. First we would hear their engines, then anti-aircraft fire, then the dull distant thuds as the bombs fell on Marples'

public house, Foster's store and the Castle Street Co-op. Joey—an
elderly budgerigar we had bought because someone had given us a cage
and it seemed a pity to waste it—seemed to develop either the gift of
prophecy or unusually acute hearing. Every time he rang his bell we
knew that the cycle—engines, guns, bombs—was about to begin again.
There was some talk of strangling Joey. But we all survived the night. I
was forbidden to crawl into the front room and see the red glow over
Shalesmoor and the Wicker, wept about it a little and fell asleep before
the "All Clear" sounded.

Airedale Road stood up pretty well to the double blitz. At number one-
hundred-and-one our only really bad moment came when Uncle Syd
brightly observed to a normally wholly unsuperstitious family that we
had all moved into Friday 13th. As he said it, we waited for Joey to ring
his bell. My worries were for the longer-term. For the thousandth time,
I asked my father to confirm that we were going to win in the end. My
father assured me that we would in a tone that sounded as if he meant it.
It was alleged by one of the patriotic young men in reserved occupations
that during an early raid a resident in the road had rushed to his gate and
cried into the night "Why don't they give in whilst there are a few of us
left?" If the story was true, by 1940 he had either regained his nerve,
reconciled himself to death or altered his strategic judgement. Like the
rest of the men he went off on the Saturday and Monday mornings to
help pull down swaying walls and shift the debris from the blocked main
roads. We had Christmas to prepare for. I got a fort, six boxes of scarlet
lead soldiers "Regiments of the British Army", and an anti-tank gun.

By the end of 1942, all the Hattersley men were in uniform. Uncle
George was a soldier. Uncle Syd was in the Air Force. My father wore the
navy-blue cap of the Police War Reserve into which he had been con-
scripted. I was resplendent in an old school blazer on to which I had
fastened every military badge I could buy, swap or steal and a pink silk
tassle that had begun life on the second-hand budgerigar's cage. I had an
army of my own, organised as autocratically as General Anders' Polish
Volunteers.

Such temporary authority as I enjoyed was attributable to my one
unique asset. My garden provided easy access to the overgrown graves in
Wadsley churchyard. Wadsley Common was, perhaps, marginally better
for manœuvres. But it was half a mile's walk and by 1943 we had grown
embarrassed about marching the streets in tin steel helmets and First
World War webbing. And the deserted churchyard was overflowing
with slime-stained jam-jars, the relics of past remembrance. Lobbed

like Mills bombs they exploded with a satisfying crash against weeping angels and broken columns.

It was young Fred Guest who stopped us. Old Fred, his grandfather, was responsible for the church itself and the roses which half-bloomed along the path that weddings and funerals trod; but he never ventured into our wilderness. Young Fred was wounded in North Africa. Whilst the holes healed, Canon George Cherry Weaver, M.A. (Oxon) gave him cigarette money in return for the removal of the twitch grass and willow-herb that flourished between the Alms Houses and Airedale Road.

Suddenly there was a real soldier wounded in a real war to talk to. We carried his scythe, dragged away the cut grass and talked about the motor-bike he would buy after the war. As he grew stronger he helped dig the new graves and we sat and watched. Ten days after he left Sheffield, somebody dug a grave for him at Anzio.

That death was more real to us than all the war that had gone before. We had lived through two blitzes and innumerable bombings. We had seen the photographs in *Picture Post* and followed our advances and retreats on the *Daily Express* map of North Africa. We had listened to broadcast speeches sandwiched between *Hi Gang!* and the sound-tracks of films starring Judy Garland and Mickey Rooney. But none of that was the real war. Having known a man shot dead by one of Hitler's bullets was. It made it impossible to play at war again.

By 1944 we were old enough to play our own small, real part. The local mental hospital—the "Wadsley" of the working men's club jokes—was converted to the needs of Normandy casualties. Boy Scouts were recruited to run errands and take messages, to collect old gramophone records and search for shops with an unlimited supply of matches.

But the reality of hospital blue and wound stripes eventually palled. No longer young enough to play at war, we had grown old enough to fantasize. Ten days before General Montgomery got the date wrong on Lüneberg Heath we decided to save the allies from a newsprint famine—a substance of which we had just learned at our new Grammar Schools. We knocked on our neighbours' doors and collected their old newspaper the day before the dustmen called. We planned a hand-over ceremony early the following morning.

My mother gave me an hour to remove the heap of old newspaper from the back garden. Some went over the wall into the churchyard that was over-grown again. As it grew dark, I threw the last few bundles into the back of the tool shed—completely covering the incendiary bomb scoop which had been broken into three pieces and left to await the end of the war in peace.

I KNEW THAT I was Labour long before I could begin to explain why it was the only possible party for me. In those early days, my unswerving affection and undying admiration was not for an ideology but for an institution. My allegiance was to dingy rooms over Co-op groceries, rusty duplicating machines which vomited dirty ink and destroyed clean paper, old ladies addressing envelopes with infinite care and obvious difficulty, piles of outdated leaflets that no one delivered and loud-speaker equipment that dented car roofs but failed to amplify the spoken word. They were all goods and chattels of the Labour Party, a family into which I had been born and for which I felt all the uncritical devotion that sons and siblings instinctively acquire.

As time and Mr Attlee's government progressed, I began to develop socialist theories to go with my Labour Party practice. From my ivory tower in the third form of the Sheffield City Grammar School, I had no doubt that they were the product of pure reason. In fact, they were the direct result of a political tradition in which I had been reared by hand. Mine was a radical reforming sort of socialism, the child of the chapels and the churches. We sang *Jerusalem* more often than *The Red Flag*. Our text and our testimony was Chapter Twenty-one of *The Revelation of Saint John*. If we were occasionally uncertain about the prospect of a new heaven, we never had doubts about our duty to build a new earth. The tradition of which I was a tiny part, changed from an aspiration into an organisation in Bradford on January 13th, 1893.

In fact, Bradford was a radical reforming city long before the Independent Labour Party chose it as the home of its first national conference. Richard Oastler, leader of the Campaign Against Yorkshire Slavery, was Steward of the Fixby Estate in Huddersfield, but his crusade began in Bradford. And it was John Wood of Bradford who compiled the careful accounts of exploitation and brutality that became the ammunition for Oastler's verbal fusillades. Wood employed children in his own factory. They worked a brief ten-hour day, were rarely strapped, attended a school for two hours every evening and saw a doctor every Tuesday morning. Oastler, Wood and the Reverend G. S. Bull of Bierley took "the factory question" into every marketplace in the West Riding, and

Michael Sadler, Member of Parliament for Aldburgh in the county of York, argued the case in the Commons for five years before it attracted the attention of the young Anthony Ashley. The result was the first inspected, and therefore first enforced, Factory Act. It prohibited the employment of children under nine. It limited the hours of labour endured by the older brothers and sisters. It proclaimed the duty of the nation to show concern and compassion for the least favoured of its citizens. Bradford's connection with that campaign is commemorated by a statue of Oastler and two of the children that he saved. And during the sixty years that followed the Factory Act for which he fought, the four great strands of British democratic socialism—evangelical non-conformism, industrial unionism, compassionate radicalism and the unquenchable belief in the improvability of man—were all woven together in the warp and weft of Bradford industry.

Bradford is what it is because of where it is. It stands in a natural basin surrounded by rising ground on which sheep once grazed. When the industrial revolution covered the hills with woollen mills rather than sheep, Bradford began to import its raw material from half the world and sell its finished cloth to all the universe. Its commitment to free trade was inevitable and absolute. When Mr Gladstone formed his first government it was an irrevocably liberal town, represented in Parliament by W. E. Forster, the most incorrigible radical in the liberal establishment.

Mr W. E. Forster, President of the Board of Education, applied to his new Education Bill all the pragmatism he believed to be an ingrained attribute of his chosen faith and adopted town. As a result, Bradford almost disowned and unseated him. The 1870 Education Act left the schools owned and run by the Catholic Church and Anglican Communion to the bishops and priests and to their congregations. Where the churches had failed and left an educational vacuum, the state would fill it. But there was to be no denominational education in the state schools, and deserving church schools were to be subsidised out of rates and taxes paid by Methodists and dissenters. Forster's plan brought universal education to England more quickly than any wholly secular scheme could possibly have done. But it set the chapels against Forster. According to Joe Chamberlain he had "thrown the education of the children of this country into the hands of the great ecclesiastical organisations which have been foremost in the obstruction of the prosperity and advancement of the nation". In fact, Forster just survived the wrath of the chapels and the scorn of Chamberlain and his statue still stands in the square which bears

CGY

his name to prove his triumph. Had he lost—as he very nearly did—he would have had only himself to blame. The influence of John Wesley is not easily overlooked in Bradford.

Drive south from Bradford to Dewsbury and it is impossible to retain any doubt about the second coming of wool and non-conformity in the nineteenth-century West Riding. In East Anglia the wealth that came from sheep built the great perpendicular parish churches of the middle ages. In Yorkshire it financed the great Victorian Methodist Chapels. Up the bank along the Manchester Road, past the rows of prosperous artisans' cottages that stand in line along the contours of the hill, every town has a mighty bethel. In Cleckheaton, the Providence Place Free Church has a massive front as solemn as a Greek temple and sides indistinguishable from a woollen mill. Two hundred yards further south, the Temperance Hall and Institute is a shrine to a no less exacting God. Three miles further on, at Heckmondwike, the Upper Chapel is just as great and equally grand. And if Forster never travelled outside the town centre to witness the place the chapels occupied in the life of Yorkshire woollen towns, he had only to visit the Wool Exchange to confirm that in the Bradford Trinity, commerce, non-conformity and liberalism were indivisible.

The Wool Exchange stands today as it stood in Forster's time, a triumph of the union of God and Mammon, chapel and state. The Wool Exchange is not splendid enough to be the cathedral of commerce, but it is clearly a church consecrated to competition. It is not even a very prepossessing church, but no one who steps inside can doubt that it is a place of worship. It was built in 1867, six years before Bradford Town Hall, and in the same venetian gothic style. But whilst the Town Hall belongs to the Victorian England of Tennyson (the Lady of Shalott might well have looked suicidally out of one of the windows in its single central tower) the Wool Exchange is essentially a celebration of the commercial rather than the chivalrous virtues.

The presiding deity, whose graven image dominates the Main Hall, is Richard Cobden. The patron saint of free trade is massive in white marble and glares out across the Exchange Floor towards the Members' Notice Board and its apparently coded telegrams—"Sydney Greasy Wool: Futures Declining: Exchange Limited". The plinth—like a stone soap-box from which he can denounce protectionism till the end of time—bears a simple legend: "Free Trade, Peace, Goodwill Amongst Nations". To the men who built the Wool Exchange virtue and self-interest coincided. They had no doubt that their creed could keep the world at peace and profit high. And they worshipped under the hammerbeam roof of the Wool Exchange with the same devout conviction that they felt in chapel on Sundays.

The Wool Exchange has come down in the world. Once it had over a thousand members. They jostled each other for a place on its floor and arranged meetings alongside its numbered red granite pillars. The pillars respect none of the conventional classical orders. Like the half-kings, half-angels that decorate the beams above them they are a strange hybrid of nineteenth-century style and Victorian vulgarity. But they are solid and dependable, built to last. In that they are typical of Bradford.

Of course some of the old habits have been modified by time. But customs have been altered rather than abandoned. St George's Hall advertises an old people's club at one of its side entrances, but it seems just as ready for a concert or oratorio as it ever was. The Alhambra theatre is now sandwiched between the red-brick Odeon and the concrete grey of the civic swimming baths and Library Theatre. But its yellow domes, white pillars and cobalt walls are as brash and brazen as when Nellie Wallace trod its boards. The Prospect Hall is now Bradford's Sikh Temple, but it is still a place of regular worship. The woollen mills have been amalgamated and rationalised, but the famous old names survive on their walls alongside the "woolmark". School-children hear fewer Old Testament quotations than once they did, but a sunken roundabout is called Jacob's Well, and they all know why.

Thrift remains a cardinal virtue, not only practised but exhibited in a city centre which must have more building societies to the square mile than any other piece of earth in England. The Huddersfield and Bradford, and the Provincial, occupy massive office blocks as high as the Town Hall Tower. The Prudential lives in staid and stately mock-Elizabethan brick at the corner of Tyrell and Baker Streets and shelters sub-offices of other societies under one of its wings. The Bradford and Bingley, the Anglia and the Leek and Westbourne seem to have branches in every street. In Bradford, those who could put something away always did. Amongst the men and women who met in 1893 to build the New Jerusalem were a good many who hoped to have a house of their own within its pearly gates.

Bradford was the natural place for the Independent Labour Party to begin its formal national existence. The town had its own Fabian Society, Trades Council and Labour Church. Twenty-three Labour Clubs flourished within its boundaries. They held lectures for the philosophically inclined, taught shorthand to prospective company clerks and formed their own orchestras. Thanks to their efforts two ILP Councillors sat in

the Town Hall, and in the General Election of 1892 Labour in Bradford
had endured the sort of defeat that has the taste of victory. Ben Tillett,
Secretary of the Dock, Wharf, Riverside and General Workers' Union,
was candidate in Bradford West. Only three Labour MPs were elected
that year—two in London and J. Havelock Wilson in Middlesbrough.
Tillett came within six hundred votes of winning.

Bradford also had W. H. Drew, strike leader at Manningham Mills,
correspondent for the radical periodicals which flourished in the West
Riding (*Yorkshire Factory Times, Bradford Labour Journal, Bradford Pioneer*)
and first President of the Bradford Labour Union. Drew had no doubt that
the ILP ought to hold its first national conference in his town. His
invitation embodied all the pugnacious self-confidence for which
Yorkshire is famous:

> Depend upon it, no executive will suit the provincials that they have no
> hand in forming. What you should set your face towards is a conference
> of provincial men and Londoners, and you cockneys ought to unbend
> and come, say to Bradford, a central town where you will find plenty
> of room for reflection.

Of course, the Independent Labour Party accepted the invitation. The
conference was held in the Labour Institute near to the place where the
strikers from Manningham Mills had assembled and been dispersed by
the police. The Institute building had started life as a Wesleyan Reform
chapel. It was captured and occupied by the Salvation Army and became
their local Citadel. The Labour Movement bought it third hand, as if
to confirm its ancient alliance with Methodism and the joyous evangelism
of crusading in city streets. The Institute was cleaned and redecorated by
its Members, for it was important that the sophisticated southern brothers
felt neither superiority nor dissatisfaction. The tables were covered with
scarlet cloth and the scene was set for the birth of the Independent Labour
Party.

All the great men of the socialist movement were there. Ben Tillett
returned to the scene of his former near glory. Bernard Shaw was aggres-
sive and argumentative. Robert Blatchford had left Bradford almost
forty years before. His mother, an itinerant actress, had abandoned the
stage in that town and walked to Halifax hand-in-hand with her infant
son to embrace prosaic poverty as a seamstress. Blatchford came back in
1893, but he arrived late. Keir Hardie was made Chairman of the Conference and ended the meeting with "Auld Lang Syne". He "started it

himself on a judiciously-pitched low note and then the delegates, all joining hands, sang the two verses with considerable precision and much heartiness". Amongst the hand-locked, low-pitched delegates was Fred Jowett, Labour Councillor and future Labour Cabinet Minister.

Fred Jowett was the sort of man who began to build the new Jerusalem brick by brick with his own hands. He began part-time work when he was eight. At thirteen, he was a full-time mill hand. Mr Forster's universal education, interrupted during infancy and abandoned in childhood, whetted an appetite which it could not satisfy. In the year that Frederick Delius left Bradford Grammar School, Fred Jowett enrolled with the Bradford Mechanics' Institute.

The "tute" had particularly Yorkshire origins. Lord Brougham's "Society for the Diffusion of Useful Knowledge" had a special appeal to the utilitarian instincts of the West Riding where they like learning to have a practical application. In some parts of the country men like George Birkbeck of Settle (his College still flourishes in London) were typical of the movement's middle-class domination. But in Bradford it was different. Back in 1825 it had been decided that "a majority of the Committee shall be artisans". It suited Jowett's needs exactly. In the Mechanics' Institute he learned enough about weaving first to become a weavers' overlooker then a manufacturer's assistant—trades with titles that illustrate the full grandeur of industrial management.

Jowett preferred the grandeur of the ILP. At twenty-eight he became a member of Bradford City Council—one of the three unexpected victories that led the way in 1892. For eight years he was Chairman of Bradford's Health Committee. Thanks to him, Bradford can boast the first school clinic, the first school dentist, the first school baths. Oastler took the children out of the factories; Forster provided them with the rudiments of education; Jowett began to give them health. And it all began in Bradford.

Fred Jowett's name passed surreptitiously into my early consciousness like Robin Hood, Richard the Lionheart and all the other boyhood heroes. My own particular personal Minister from Mr MacDonald's Government was A. V. Alexander, Labour and Co-operative Member of Parliament for the Hillsborough Division of Sheffield, a man with a waistcoat and a watch-chain, the sort of collar affected by lay-preachers and known to the profane as "come to Jesus", and false teeth that slipped when required to wrestle with a series of sibilants. I held him in absolute awe. No doubt he had a Christian name. But it never seemed to me that I was entitled even to imagine what his mother called him. Such intimacy with the likes of him was not permitted to the likes of me.

A. V. Alexander was First Lord of the Admiralty. Fred Jowett would not have approved. His uncompromising pacifism cost him two Parliamentary Elections. He lost West Bradford by forty-one votes in 1900 at the height of anti-Boer jingoism. In 1918, when the land fit for heroes was about to be built just as soon as the Kaiser was hanged and Germany was squeezed until the pips squeaked, he fought East Bradford on a manifesto dedicated to brotherly love. He lost again. But I never saw any conflict or paradox in Jowett and Alexander serving the same party. I knew that in the Labour Party there were many mansions, each occupied by a different sort of socialist. That is how it was in Hillsborough in 1948. No doubt it was much the same in Bradford in 1893.

The ILP delegates who arrived on January 13th at Bradford's two great railway stations (Forster Square still thrives, but Exchange only survives as two gothic arches of glass and girders that mark the boundary of a municipal car park) were as mixed a bunch as today's Labour Party. They argued about ways and disagreed about means of achieving their common objective. They argued their way through the Conference and on into the twentieth century and they kept on arguing until they returned to Bradford in 1936 and agreed to merge into the bigger and better argument of the Labour Party itself. Between 1945 and 1950 that Party changed the history of Great Britain. It nationalised the mines, it built the health service and it made India free. They were five years of genuinely radical government. And it all began in Bradford in 1893.

LIMESTONE COUNTRY

LIMESTONE MAKES complicated country—complicated in size, shape, colour and contour. That is because it dissolves in water. So instead of the rain running along its surface in dull rivers, it tunnels mysterious passages where the limestone ends and the less soluble rock begins. Sometimes the subterranean streams burst out in sudden waterfalls. Sometimes they cut caves so broad and deep that the rock above collapses and a new valley appears in the landscape. And if, in some prehistoric age, the soft limestone and the hard slate and grit that nature laid below it, were folded, buckled and broken by a mighty earthquake and then cut and carved by a passing glacier the result is one of the natural wonders of the world.

That is exactly what happened at the head of the Yorkshire dales across a great sweep of country that runs from Ingleton and the Lune in the west to Pen-y-Ghent and the Ribble in the east. Lying between, near where the Aire begins below Fountains Fell is Malham Tarn, a delight to geologists, botanists and ornithologists. And to those who wish neither to count the number of different birds nor catalogue the various species of flowers, it is simply the most beautiful place in England.

Malham Tarn is a huge high lake, twelve hundred feet above the sea, held up by a massive slab of slate and kept in by a pile of grit and gravel that a glacier left behind on Malham Lings. Twice, during the age before the Pennines were finally formed, the land split open and along the Craven Faults a hundred miles of Yorkshire sank towards the warm centre of the world. So in the wooded hills and crevassed crags which surround the tarn, there are places where the millstone grit and Bowland shale show through. But despite the confusions of shape and the complexities of substance it is the limestone which stands out, starkly white in a green countryside.

Sometimes it appears in great scars, the remains of the long wall of limestone left by the Craven Fault and now broken down into isolated cliffs by ten thousand years of erosion. Sometimes it breaks out of the surrounding fells and creates dappled steps—vertically white dotted with clumps of green grass and horizontally green freckled with loose white boulders. And where there are continuous sweeps of coarse, rough grass, the limestone walls mark boundaries between the fields with a crazy irregularity of triangles and polygons. Limestone is not Malham's only miracle. There are the dark woods that run down to its northern shore. On its western horizon is a great v-shaped valley cut with irresistible precision by the waters which flowed south when the ice age melted. Between Highfolds and Great Close Scars, the grey-green grass that covers the hills is sprinkled with wild thyme and hare-bells. But it is the limestone that makes Malham unforgettable.

> If it is this landscape that we the inconstant ones,
> Are constantly homesick for, this is chiefly
> Because it dissolves in water.

When, in 1951, I first visited Malham Tarn I was only interested in its physical geography. It was the year of Higher School Certificate and one paper of my examination was to be solely concerned with the shape and size of the surface of England and why the wolds and the downs and the dales were there. Within an area easily reached by bus from Ingleton were examples of everything that had ever happened to the face of Britain. So off our party of sixth form geographers went to see it at first hand. I recorded our visit (by-line: Roy S. G. Hattersley 6u) in the school magazine. The article ended with a memorable valedictory paragraph that at least proved that my reaction to limestone country was not plagiarised from W. H. Auden:

> This was a geographical trip [it was a more innocent age, when the word had no psychedelic implications] and was conducted as such. However, it is not for the author—were he able—to give an account of glacially striated Silurian erratics, uniformly perched upon clinted limestone pavements, of incised rejuvenated streams, of notches and terraces, of faults and intrusions, but rather to tell of an enjoyable holiday for which the party offers its sincere thanks to both the management of the *Hollin Tree* and to Mr Hodge.

That expedition introduced me to Malham, but that is not the result of which I was immediately most conscious. I arrived in Ingleton certain of my physical fitness. I left with severe doubts about my health and strength. Three great peaks, Whernside (2400 feet), Pen-y-Ghent (2200 feet) and Ingleborough (2300 feet) are spread across the countryside at the three points of an isosceles triangle—part of what was the Pennine arch, a great fold of rock pushed up towards the sky and then worn down by frost and rain into a dozen mountains and a hundred hills. To the heroic they offer a single day's challenge—great Whernside before breakfast, Ingleborough in the morning, Pen-y-Ghent during the afternoon, and the victorious name of the successful fell walker in the book kept by Settle Church before supper. I never even aspired to that, but I did expect to climb a peak a day with ease.

I climbed a peak each day but it was never easy. The hard fell grass was as slippery as it was coarse and slid away under leather shoes. Every full pace forward was diminished by a half slide back, so every step involved special effort. All the hills (and particularly Pen-y-Ghent, like a great sandcastle with towers and tunnels worn down by the sea and, according to Wordsworth, "seldom free from wind or frost or vapours wet") offered false hope. From the little plateaux that provided comfort at the top of every slope it always looked as if the next ascent would be the last. Yet time after time, at the top of the apparently last climb, there was apparently just one climb more. I struggled to the top of each hill and placed my stone on the cairn that marked the highest point, jubilant that my lump of rock was the highest spot on the map but sad to think that by tomorrow a dozen little boulders would be piled above it. From the flat crown of Ingleborough, looking over the earthworks which were once the outer ramparts of a Brigantine stronghold, I could see Blackpool Tower and the great viaduct at Ribblehead. South was Yorkshire and the beginning of the dales.

According to the guide-books, the Dales begin at Skipton. Perhaps to the tourist they do. But the Wharfe rises between Whernside and Pen-y-Ghent, the Ribble runs east of Ingleton and only turns from a stream into a river when Ingleborough waters join it, and the source of the Aire is less than five miles south of Fountains Fell. That is the visible water of the limestone country. Underground there is another world of caves, caverns and potholes. At God's Bridge, just below Chapel-le-Dale, the river Twiss emerges into the sunlight and flows on above the ground to join the Greta. At Gaping Gill, the stream suddenly disappears and continues on its mysterious subterranean way, three hundred and sixty-five feet under the valley floor. Gingle Pot and Hurtle Pot are steep vertical shafts, like air ducts in a mine. There is water at the bottom of both. That can be confirmed by dropping a pebble down. It will make a splash —after a long pause.

The holes that nature has drilled into the limestone country go deep. And the limestone cliffs (being the part of the great slab of limestone that was broken and pushed up to stand out on the landscape like the sides of King Solomon's mines) once rose up to the same three hundred feet as the pots descend. Since the earth broke and the edge of the limestone was first exposed, wind and weather have worn some of them away. The climbers that toil up the scars east of Malham Tarn have less than three hundred feet to pull and heave. Most of the great white crags that line the roads between Grassington and Arncliffe Cole and from Settle north-west out of the county to Kirkby Lonsdale have been half washed or worn away. But there are two great walls of stone—majestic on a sunny day, menacing in the rain—which are almost complete from top to bottom. Malham Cove is part of the great white gash cut into the landscape and called, ten thousand years after the land moved, the Craven Fault. Gordale Scar (as high but not so steep) is what was left after the water dug too deep and the cavern roof collapsed. The beck provides a damp pathway for those daring or daft enough to make the descent to the place where Turner sat below the Scar and recognised from its sparkling water and shiny stone the need to paint light as well as the objects on which it falls. In 1951 I was daft enough to do anything that I was dared. I scrambled down Gordale Scar. I played hopscotch across the limestone which spread out above Malham Cove like a giant slab of white chocolate, half separated into blocks and ready to be broken piece by piece. And having failed to break my leg that way, I set out to prove that I could climb faster and walk further than any of my peers. As I remember the unnecessary contest, I lost in both events. But I did have one magnificent victory. I had seen Malham Tarn and the memory of it was firmly engraved on my mind.

It was almost twenty years before—in remembering it—I realised how beautiful it was. Then I could not stay away. On a north country mission for the Ministry of Labour I played truant for half a day and watched the ripple of its water. On a dull afternoon at a Blackpool Labour Party Conference I tricked a colleague with a car into driving me across Lancashire to its western shore. In the summer of 1975 I arrived again, an amateur visitor amongst the conscious professionalism of the thick socks, studded boots and cantilever rucksacks of the Pennine Way. It was just the same. At the gateway of the Field Study Centre there was a box of leaflets with fascinating details of the fish and flowers I could expect in August.

> ... Dear, I know nothing of
> Either, but when I try to imagine a faultless love
> Or the life to come, what I hear is the murmur
> Of underground streams, what I see is a limestone landscape.

THREE

Go East Young Man

Hull and I came together as the result of our mutual insecurity. Until 1951 the City and Port was nothing more to me than the place—along with Hell and Halifax—from which pious Yorkshiremen prayed for deliverance. But all that ended on the February morning when the letter from C. R. Meggitt, Registrar, was pushed through our door.

The University College of Hull—then still part of an academic empire ruled from Senate House in London—was anxious for independence and was convinced that an increase in student numbers would reinforce its application for a Charter of its own. Faced with the competition of longer established institutions (and hamstrung by the current myth that only a tiny proportion of the population could sustain a university education) the University College determined to make the earliest bids in the undergraduate market. That is not exactly how C. R. Meggitt, Registrar, described the early offer of a place. But I make no complaint about the slight deception. Had I known the truth, nothing would have changed. I felt sure that a Higher School Certificate was within my grasp, but confident belief would only be changed into established fact after the anxieties of a whole summer. I wanted certainty, and certainty of a sort Hull could provide. Two hours after we had torn the letter open, we phoned the University College and left a message for C. R. Meggitt, Registrar, himself. In short I said yes to the first man who asked me, just in case I was never asked again. The episode says little for my self-confidence, but it is a perfect example of my continual good luck. After a difficult first few days we settled down to enjoy the rest of a natural span together. I, at least, have no regrets.

I left for Hull at eight o'clock on the morning of the first Monday in October. Harry Colley—by then a furnaceman but legendary in Wadsley because, in his youth, he had auditioned for Covent Garden and played for Yorkshire Colts—was at the Worrall Road bus stop in clogs, cloth cap and sweat-rag. He assumed that, as I was going to Hull, I was going to sea and warned me that it would be a hard life. Settled in a corner of the old-fashioned sort of railway carriage, I felt sure that the more sophisticated cross-country passengers would tell the difference between an undergraduate and a seaman. For thirty miles we puffed north—

Rotherham, Mexboro, Conisbrough, Thorne and Goole. Then, we swung east—Brough, Ferriby, Hessle and Hull. For the last half hour we ran alongside the Humber, travelling in reverse the line that Philip Larkin took when he was late getting away for the Whitsun Weddings:

> We ran behind the backs of houses, crossed a street,
> Of blinding windscreens, smelt the fish-dock, then
> The river's level drifting breadth began,
> Where sky and Lincolnshire and water meet.

A boyhood spent in the Pennine foothills had not prepared me for Hull. As I stepped outside the Paragon Station the flatness of the place struck me like an unsuccessful pancake. The roads from Paragon Square shot out in thin straight lines covering the shortest distances between the city, its docks and the market towns of the East Riding. I knew that I had come to the place where England ended, that after this, there could only be sea. Behind me was the real Yorkshire of hills and valleys where the roads climbed and bent. Ahead there was nothing but water; and that was only one degree better than empty space.

As I came to know Hull I came to accept, if not enjoy, its flatness and all the strange manifestations of the horizontal life. I chased the trolley buses, walked the footpaths parallel to the storm dykes Hull called drains, joined the massed ranks of pedal-cyclists who never laboured up hill but never free-wheeled down, and waited—"on bus or foot or bike"—at the railway level-crossings' gates that bisect every Hull main road. I came from a land of viaducts, cuttings and tunnels and never grew wholly reconciled to life in a two-dimensional city. But I adjusted to it. It was a small price to pay for the other boons and benefits.

For the first year, life in the University College was so absorbing that I never saw the town at all. I lived outside the city boundary in Cottingham, birthplace of Winifred Holtby and home of the Haltemprice Rural District Council, where the University College had chosen to house its students amongst the market gardens. Everything outside my life in college was no more than an extension of my life within it. On my Christmas train journey to hear the *Messiah* sung in Beverley, I was just one long blue-and-yellow scarf in a carriage full of long blue-and-yellow scarves. Inside the freezing Minster I was protected from frostbite of the knee by one Hall of Residence blanket in a row of Hall of Residence blankets. Journeys to a school at Withernsea, a village green at Bishop Burton, an airfield at Pocklington, were made in exclusive University

College buses to play for exclusively University College teams. Instead of enjoying real films in real cinemas, I endured the elderly artistry of Film Soc. I abandoned the real Labour Party for the dialectic attractions of Lab. Soc. and Soc. Soc. When I caused mayhem at Hull Fair, it was carefully organised University College mayhem. My world was very beautiful and very small.

It began to expand when I left the protected (though uncloistered) Hall of Residence and moved into lodgings. In the back bedroom of 125 Blenheim Street, I could feel the earth tremble as the early morning trains rushed cod and haddock to the industrial midlands. At the first trace of mist the persistent notes of the Humber foghorns would intrude into our Sunday evening darts and interrupt our endless arguments. When the wind blew north, the smell of the Fish Dock would swirl through the backyard and into the kitchen. Suddenly I understood that Hull was about the sea not the land. It was there because, in an earlier age, the ocean had been its benefactor. By 1955 the tide had gone out.

Once the signs of maritime life were inescapable. The first dock Britain built outside London was dug in Hull in 1774. It remained in the centre of the city for over a hundred and fifty years until it was filled in, dried out and transformed from Queen's Dock into Queen's Garden. It is a green oasis in an architectural desert.

Hull's civic buildings were designed at unhappy times and in unlovely styles. There was something genuinely gothic and imperial about Victoria's England. The great municipal buildings that the Queen and her consort opened represented the true spirit of the time. By the end of King Edward's reign, the confidence that characterised the age of hope was beginning to fade. Instead of a commitment to change and improvement, there was the desire to keep the world as it was. The cities that had not yet built their public monuments copied the patterns of past achievement as economically as they could. Hull Town Hall carried all the scars of 1906—an interior strangely like its namesake's in Leeds and shops built into its outside walls to ensure that the £100,000 it cost to build made a contribution to commerce as well as to culture.

The Guildhall and Law Courts (two architects, three stages, ten years and £160,000) were finished during the year when 400,000 British soldiers died in the battle of the Somme as the price Field Marshal Haig was prepared to pay for six miles of muddy ground. On the left flank of the Fourth Army stood the 31st Division. Within its ranks were the 10th, 11th, 12th and 13th Battalions of the East Riding Regiment—the Hull Commercials, the Hull Tradesmen, the Hull Sportsmen and T'others.

Those who returned to a Hull fit for heroes to live in found Alfred Gelder Street transformed. The new Guildhall was complete. Two maritime Boadiceas held their tridents aloft above its mock-classical façade as if the year was something to celebrate.

Twenty-five years later the Second World War came directly and terribly to Hull. No English city was bombed more heavily or more often, and the planes that pounded the docks would not or could not draw the line which divided the City and Port of Kingston upon Hull. In 1951, when I stepped out of Paragon Station, there were still great gaping holes in what had once been the town centre. They were filled, during the next ten years, by a strange combination of concrete and a revival of the Regency classical revival. As a result, Hull is one of the few cities where shoe shops and electricity showrooms shine their neon signs from below Corinthian columns.

But buried behind the Hull Hofbräuhaus and hard by Hammond's store are glimpses of what Hull used to be. Hull had a tradition that lasted a thousand years. The hope of finding something new and the determination to get there first stretched from the day that St Willibrod left his cave at the mouth of the Humber to the moment Amy Johnson touched her plane down in Australia. Once it was a trading city, a place to which people came expecting to buy and sell and prosper. Robinson Crusoe's father landed at Hull from Bremen and settled there before he moved inland to York. It was the great port of the middle ages and the magnificent mercantile city of Tudor and Stuart England. Inevitably it was for the Protector against the Pope and the Commonwealth against the King. John Hotham closed the city gates against the Duke of York in 1642 and the Civil War began. A year later Sir Thomas Fairfax and his Yorkshire Puritans held the East Riding for the Parliament from the citadel inside Hull's city walls. Hull was firmly against ship money and in favour of the Thirty-nine Articles and the signs of its commercial and radical past are all around.

Prince's Dock runs hard by Victoria Square, bringing small ships into the city centre as great were brought in when the Queen's Dock flourished. In the Market Place a gilded King Billy sits astride his horse surrounded by shops that sell potatoes and stalls which auction peas. But he is there to confirm that in England Kings rule only with the consent of Parliament, and that those who proclaim their providential rights will not prosper in the East Riding. Holy Trinity Church has a chancel built of brick as old as any brick in England and is tall and fine because prosperity and piety once went hand and hand in Yorkshire. Trinity House—erected in 1753,

two hundred and fifty years after the guild of mariners was founded—
is a tribute to Georgian architecture and to seamanship as a craft. The walls
of Wilberforce House bulge with relics of the trade which the Member
of Parliament for Hull did more to end than any man in England. It is
testimony both to the compassionate Christianity that brought slavery to
an end and to the part that human purchase played in building the
prosperity of the eighteenth-century Empire. Whitefriargate and Delapole
Avenue are memorials to the monks and merchants who built the old
city between the Hull and the Humber. The Land of Green Ginger is a
reminder that in the days of sail and scurvy (before Captain Cook, the
coal-barge skipper from up the coast in Whitby, had perfected English
navigation) sailors only put to sea if they were incurably romantic or
desperately hungry.

I was neither, so despite my years in Hull, I never set foot on a sensible
ship or sailed on a serious ocean. I did, however, make constant, pointless,
beautiful trips across the Humber and back on the British Railway Ferry.
The Ferry berthed, at the Yorkshire end of its journey, against the Victoria
Pier. Waiting for its arrival on the top tier of the (now sadly demolished)
two-storey jetty, prospective passengers could look out on a whole royal
family of docks. To the west was the Albert. To the east were the Victoria,
the Alexandra and the King George. Each embraced mighty ships carrying
mighty cargoes.

They did not interest me. I squinted out across the iron-grey Humber
looking for the first sign that the ferry had left New Holland. It approached
Hull in a great arc, half steaming, half drifting with the tide. It was
squat, dirty and inhospitable. But despite all that, I passed some of my
happiest moments standing on its deck or edging my way between the
tethered motor cars to its lower saloon and bars. I watched the water
ripple by and thought great thoughts and had new ideas as Lincolnshire
approached and Yorkshire receded. On the way back the thoughts were
still greater and the ideas even newer than those which had changed the
world on the outward journey.

The Hull ferry will, of course, disappear. As the new bridge brings life
and vitality to Hull it will become obsolete, a ritual sacrifice to progress.
Then Hull will have its second coming with its deep-sea fleet freezing
the catch almost before it is in the net and the containerised cargoes filling
the rosters of the new merchant fleet to bursting point. Let us hope all that
really happens, and that Hull (always a slightly hungry-looking town even
when the trawlers are home and the expensive presents are pushed to the
front of the cheap shop windows) grows prosperous again. But for me,

even when it is no longer the end of the line but a thriving port joined by land and sea to solvency and Europe, I shall think of it as the place where the ferry ties up.

To me, the ferry stands for the best books I ever read (neither required nor recommended; just enjoyed), the first real ideas I ever had, and the best friends I ever made. The years on the ferry were the best three out of my first twenty-one. God bless you C. R. Meggitt, Registrar.

WISH YOU WERE HERE

I WAS BORN in industrial south Yorkshire in the 1930s so it was only to be expected that, if my parents could afford a holiday at all, my first week at the seaside would be spent at Bridlington in a boarding house. Those seven days are the beginning of my memory. They are now over-laid by almost forty years of new faces, fresh incidents, essential informa-tion and useless statistics. But little bits of Bridlington 1936 still push themselves to the front of my mind—the taste of rubber, sand and salt-water combined into the single experience of blowing up a beach ball; a celluloid deep-sea diver who sank and surfaced in a basin of water; the tin binoculars we left on the beach and recovered two days and four tides later; the deep-sea monsters, pickled, bottled and displayed by part of an amusement arcade which called itself a maritime museum. Say "summer holiday" and they are all regurgitated from the place in my brain where eventful and extraordinary experiences are stored.

In fact it was a wholly commonplace holiday. I did all the things that four-year-olds do at the seaside. I built sand-castles too near to the sea, tempted by the wet sand that made building easy. For the first time in my life (though regrettably by no means the last) I saw my work collapse because I was tempted by the easy route to success. I watched Punch and Judy with an absolute inability to suspend infant disbelief. But at the Church Army's "Sunshine Corner" I suffered neither doubt nor un-certainty. Jesus bade *me* shine with clear, pure light. I sang away shining as purely and clearly as I possibly could.

For my parents it was a holiday of anxieties. There was a chronically sick grandmother at home and a desperate shortage of spending money by the sea. Whenever we passed the miniature railway I expected to travel on it. Every time we saw a horse-drawn landau (still a feature of the Bridlington summer) I expected to ride in it. I needed ice-creams and packets of paper flags on wire that could be stuck in sand-castle turrets. Above all, I longed for constant trips on the pleasure steamers. I wanted to sail on the *Yorkshireman* and the *Princess Marina*, to sit on their rear decks, watch the sea rush past their stern propellers and listen to the wind-up gramophone playing the tunes of the moment. It was my first acquain-tance with the incomparable popular music of the thirties. It captivated my young mind and captured my tender soul. Since then there has been no room for Bartók or Shostakovich in a musical memory joyously filled with Gershwin, Porter, Berlin and Rogers. And I can recall exactly where the passion began. To this day I have only to hear *Cheek to Cheek* or *September in the Rain* to be back on the *Yorkshireman*, somewhere in Bridlington Bay.

Benefiting from the prosperity that came with the end of the war, our summer holidays began slowly to move up the coast. The further north we got the higher we had risen in the world, for Yorkshire resorts gained social status with latitude. Furthest south of all (further south even than Bridlington) was Withernsea, with the lighthouse in its main street as its only distinction. One up from Withernsea was Hornsea, a pretty village where the great fresh-water mere has sedge enough to give it an air of Arthurian doom, but hardly a place to make first choice for a fortnight's relaxation. Next was Bridlington and after Bridlington Filey, which in 1945 specialised in the respectable suburbs which found Scarborough just too expensive. After Filey there was just Scarborough to hope for. It was not the northernmost of Yorkshire's holiday towns. But beyond, there was only quaint and quirky Whitby, too complicated and confused to be allocated a very precise place in the seaside social register.

The world has changed since those post-war years. It has grown more prosperous and more adventurous and many of its exotic places are now within the reach and expectations of families who, fifty years ago, would have saved up all the year for a day beside the seaside. The Yorkshire resorts have responded to the change not by catering for the poorest holiday maker (for a week on the Costa Brava can be provided more cheaply than a week in Cayton Bay) but by meeting the wishes of people who really want their holidays to be like a Donald McGill postcard, and the needs of families with too many children to take the long package trail to Spain and the sun.

Scarborough has given the lead in meeting the needs of the young. Critics might argue that Scarborough has gone down in the world. Scarborough will insist that the world has gone down around it and that is why respectable hotels like the Cliff Inn have to display signs which read "Bedrollers and persons wearing leather jackets will not be admitted to this establishment". But all the young are not equally unwelcome. In the Royal Hotel, beneath the splendid triple galleries which encircle the foyer's classical pillars in wrought-iron splendour, two notices are prominently displayed: "Wed. Children's Party Night" and "Fri. Children's Hour". High on the third deck—where drawings of the Great

Exhibition depict such important displays as Japan, Russia, the German Zollverein and Green Lane Works, Sheffield—the white-painted balustrades are paralleled by high glass screens in case adolescents should plunge to their death as they giggle down to Monday night's teenage disco in the Neptune Ballroom.

Filey seems hardly to have changed. I spent teenage summers there, old enough to appreciate the sweeping bay as well as enjoy the endless sands. Indeed, I was growing out of sand and had begun to realise that holidays at the sea did not have to be exclusively concerned with maritime matters. I read Kitto's *The Greeks* and Eileen Powers' *Medieval People* and found them compelling as well as compulsory holiday reading. I played tennis on the inland municipal courts, clothed in the glory of my first real tennis shorts which had at last replaced the Royal Navy surplus which had previously hung about my knees. Every match was a Wimbledon Final, part of the fantasy world which I inhabited for long stretches of my life, before politics appeared and proved that reality can be exciting too. But if I neglected the beach, Dinah our four-year-old half-Labrador did not. Dinah had her own fantasy—a belief that she could catch birds. Having tip-toed across the cracked and crevassed stones of Filey Brig she would tear across the sand, leaping a speculative three feet into the air in the certain belief that she could savage seagulls flying thirty yards above. I admired her indomitable optimism and envied her joy in defecation. Nature's work done, she would kick her back legs in the air and spray grass from the sand-dunes behind her like winnowed chaff. I sat, uncomfortably, in the Elsan shed behind our wooden bungalow and longed to experience the same elation.

Whitby, of course, came later. We stayed in a cottage in the old town, a muddle of small red and grey houses piled on top of each other against the face of the East Cliff. From my bedroom window I could look out across the harbour and see the working fishing boats moored against the quay. The same boats still seem to be there, but now they are tied up in front of *The Harbour Diner* and *Funland—Bingo and Amusements*, and create the composite picture of modern Whitby. The town is half Victorian fishing village, half day-trippers' delight; a place where, when the smell of fish ends, the smell of fish 'n chips begins.

West Whitby, with its broad sands and spa and what were once elegant hotels, was obviously a premier summer attraction in a less sophisticated age—an age when the city fathers could call one of the roads leading to Captain Cook's statue the Khyber Pass as a straightforward tribute to the Indian Empire. The gaunt Victorian hotels of

West Whitby, looking down on the natural habour and the jetties and sea walls that make it an even safer haven, enjoy a perfect view of St Mary's Church and Whitby Abbey high on the opposite bank of the Esk. In my days at Whitby, visitors approached the Abbey penitentially up the hundred and ninety steps of Jacob's ladder and performed the whole pilgrimage with appropriate reverence. Now there is a car park under the monastic walls and visitors, having arrived in ease, enjoy the Abbey in comfort. On hot afternoons, men lie shirtless on the close-cropped grass and shield their eyes from sun that shines through where the roof would have been if Henry had not dissolved the monasteries.

Yorkshire abounds in ruined monasteries, the result of the Reformation and four hundred years of neglect, but St Mary's, Whitby, is unique at least in England. Its roof—built by ships' carpenters like a ship's deck with window hatches that provide light for the congregation down in the hold—is probably the only one of its sort anywhere in the world. But the New England white wooden galleries and the high pews are a familiar sight in Massachusetts. Inside, St Mary's is a Cape Cod whalers' church. From its porch *Funland* and *The Harbour Diner* are clearly visible.

Bridlington always has been and always will be a place where funlands and diners grow in such profusion that no individual arcade or café actually holds the attention. I played my first pin-ball machine in Bridlington, grabbed at my first glass trinket with my first mechanical hand and got my first cheap thrill by watching the working model of the gallows almost until the trap dropped and Crippen dangled at the end of a rope. That is what I did on the one dismally wet half day of my first holiday.

Bridlington is not at its breezy best on rainy days. Even in the self-assured seventies, its streets still appear to be filled with families who cannot or dare not return to their digs before six o'clock. They huddle against trees and in shop doorways, crowd under awnings or simply walk about getting wet. Yet they appear to remain incredibly cheerful, indomitably enjoying their holiday, a standing reproof to tourists on the Côte d'Azur whose day is spoilt when the white wine is not chilled. Their habits and their humour spread for miles around. They enliven damp afternoons in Sewerby Park, when the ladies orchestra has retired from the bandstand and the long-bows are too wet for amateur archers to hold. They stand at the pavement's edge and watch the shivering donkeys trotting home. They queue outside Flamborough lighthouse, waiting their turn to climb its interminable stairs, so that they can look out from the lamp platform and enjoy a visibility of virtually nil.

Below them, lost in the mist, is the North Landing, protected from the waves by the biggest breakwater in England, Flamborough Head. The landing is simply a narrow strip of sand. Between the cliffs that run out at right-angles to the land lies what passes for calm water at Flamborough. For despite the snack bar and the shop that sells plastic star fish, Flamborough is the sea, not the seaside.

It epitomises the Yorkshire of steep cliffs and rough water—the Yorkshire with its lifeboats ready to put to sea. In Bridlington the lifeboat stands on the promenade. At one minute it is a tourist attraction welcoming visitors into its little booth like the innumerable Gipsy Petulengros. At the next it is bouncing across the waves on its way to drag men and cargoes back to dry land. For lifeboatmen, not every journey can end in front of a cottage fire, pulling off oilskins and drinking mugs of rum-laced tea. On February 9th, 1861, Mr Keane wrote from Whitby to *The Times*:

We have had a fearful storm today. Half a mile of our strand is already strewn with seven wrecks; a new lifeboat launched a few months ago was manned by the finest picked seamen of Whitby. Five times during the day they have braved the furious sea and five times returned from the vessels in distress. A sixth ship was driven behind the pier. The men, exhausted though they were, again pulled out, but, before they had gone fifty yards, a wave capsized the boat. Then was beheld by several thousand persons, within almost a stone's throw but unable to assist, the fearful agonies of those powerful men, buffeting with the fury of the breakers till, one by one, twelve out of thirteen sank, and only one was saved. There were ten widows, forty-four fatherless children and two dependants.

At Flamborough the lifeboat proudly displays the lists of ships rescued and lives saved; three hundred and ninety-three souls taken from the sea with much the same risks as Grace Darling up in Northumberland and Ham Peggotty down in Norfolk faced a hundred years ago.

Down the steep steps that lead past the lifeboat house to the edge of the North Sea very little has changed since the British fleet fought the new American navy off Flamborough in 1779. That was a bad year for maritime Yorkshire. Forty miles up the coast, within sight of Scarborough, John Paul Jones made his name by sinking British merchantmen. On the other side of the world, James Cook, sometime apprentice haberdasher of Staithes, sometime coal barge captain, was killed in Hawaii. Since then several tons of rock have fallen into the sea and the caves have dug deeper into the land. But Flamborough is basically the same as it always was and all the better for it.

On the road above, the refugees from Butlin's hitch-hike past in search of less regimented pleasures than their camps provide. They are part of Yorkshire's new east coast. All the way from Whitby Abbey in the north, up the Victorian staircase of the Royal at Scarborough, over Filey Brig and on to the irrepressible weekly boarders of Bridlington it is impossible to argue that what has lasted longest is not the best.

OUT OF SEASON

IT TOOK ME eighteen years to get to Scarborough. As a child my week of summer holiday was spent in Bridlington or Mablethorpe. When a youth, I made the more adventurous journey overland to Morecambe. Scarborough was beyond us—the holiday to which the Yorkshire working class aspired but rarely attained. For Scarborough was posh. It had hotels of the sort that Bridlington could never boast. It had a castle as a sign of antiquity and a cricket festival to prove that even Yorkshire can descend to genteel frivolity once the season is over and the Championship justly won or unfairly lost. It had the artificial waterfalls of Peasholm Park and electric lifts—called tramways—to carry the infirm or indolent holiday maker from the edge of the sea to the top of the cliff. Above all, it had a Spa, the relic of an earlier elegance which had left a permanent mark of class on the town.

Yet, although I always knew that Scarborough was different, the details of its distinction were denied me until the afternoon in August 1952 when, with my parents, I stepped down from a bus labelled "Valley Parade Terminus". Below us was the valley itself, a ravine running from the East Riding to the sea dividing the South Bay from the old town and the North Bay beyond. We ate our sandwiches on the steep slopes of the Valley Gardens and agreed that Scarborough was a very special place.

It is, in fact, three places. That day we saw one of them—the old town where real people live all the year round, serving the transient summer trade but keeping Scarborough a place distinct in itself. The North Bay and its endless promenade (parts of which are too respectable to bear a name redolent of rock and candy floss and are, therefore, known as the Royal Albert and Marine Drives) were hidden from our bench in Valley Gardens by the castle rock—a huge lump of oolitic limestone the size of a Pennine foothill and the shape of a Victorian door-knob which sticks out into the North Sea. By the time we had climbed to where the Romans had built their warning beacons and looked out across the ruins of the Norman Keep and Angevin Castle it was time to catch the bus back to Whitby. I did not return to Scarborough for ten years. For my second visit I travelled by car from Sheffield, concentrating on the complicated diversions which took me round the walls of York and on the stern political business which brought me to the East Coast. On Sunday, October 2nd, 1960, I began to find out about Scarborough's South Bay and its Spa.

In the sixties, at the end of every second summer, when the holiday tide had finally gone out and the last of the sand-castles had been washed away, the Labour Party moved into Scarborough. Then for five days every housemaid and hall porter, every taxi-driver and boarding-house landlady, looked for patronage and custom to the Spa. The institution which they eyed with commercial hope and political apprehension had bubbled forth its benevolent waters for a thousand years. In the seventeenth century the mineral spring had been adjudged to restore health and promote vitality. By the beginning of the eighteenth, the Spa House was attracting society as well as the sick. Fifty years later, when watering places were really coming into fashion and Lord Foppington conceded that "even the bores of the northern Spas have learned to respect a title", Scarborough (together with Harrogate) was as near as Yorkshire got to the saline sophistication of Bath and Brighton. Indeed, the Spa still has the lingering air of a place which provides a pleasure for the prosperous. But the middle-class ghosts who haunt its bars and promenades take their pleasures in moderation. The water in the pump room may sparkle, but they do not.

That is, in part, the product of the Yorkshire character—the belief that pleasure is a serious business justified at the Spa by its connection with the laudable pursuit of health and longevity. But that is not the only reason. The Spirit of the Spa owes much to the location, and consequent history, of the building.

Scarborough has a long history of attempts to enshrine its liquid asset in an appropriate temple. None of the shrines lasted for long. The health-giving waters gushed out at the foot of the South Cliff, twenty yards above the mark of high tide. So every structure that was built over and around it was particularly vulnerable to storm and landslip. In the decades when the pump rooms were engulfed by neither earth nor water they were consumed by fire. The catalogue of disaster continued well into the nineteenth century. In 1858, Joseph Paxton—having progressed from head gardener at Chatsworth to creator of the world's largest greenhouse at Crystal Palace—designed a conservatory as an extension to the fifth building in the long line of architectural achievements and natural disasters. Of course, it all burned down. But at least that nineteenth-century cataclysm did not bring with it the catastrophe which accompanied the eighteenth-century landslip. In 1737 the movement of earth was so great that the spring itself disappeared for almost half a century. After the fire of 1876, a determined and industrious corporation could begin to rebuild the Spa at once. The fashion for drinking bitter water was in decline; but the ballroom, the bandstand and the music-hall were in the ascendant. The new Spa was designed to include all three; standing in line at the foot of the South Cliff, a cricket pitch's length away from the sea.

It stands there still, touched only lightly by time; heavy and expensive, the product of an age not of hope but certainty. Yet, for all the assurance of its period and all the confidence of its design, it looks about as secure as a wooden hut on the slopes of Mount Vesuvius. On a wet and windy day, it seems inconceivable that the Spa will survive. If the sea does not wash it away, it will be engulfed in stone—not simply crumbling oolitic limestone, but the rubble from the great grey hotels on the Esplanade above, which are certain to slide into the sea with the South Cliff when the great inevitable landslide begins.

It was in that forbidding building in the shadow of apparently imminent destruction that the Labour Party appropriately gathered on October 3rd, 1960. Almost a year before, the forty-eighth Annual Conference had assembled at Blackpool, seven weeks after the Party's third consecutive election defeat. No matter how great the idealism and devotion of its members, a political party can go on losing only for so long. The growing suspicion that carrying the gospel to the heathen will no longer produce mass conversion turns an evangelical movement in upon itself. Supposed heretics are denounced. Apostates are excommunicated. Points of obscure internal theology are elevated to questions of the utmost principle. So it was in the Labour Party between Blackpool 1959 and Scarborough 1960. Mounting despair and growing disagreement combined to produce convulsions that looked ominously like death throes.

Many observers genuinely believed that the last mortal agony would be witnessed on the afternoon of October 5th. Then—it was pre-ordained by votes promised before they were cast—the Labour Party would commit itself in favour of unilateral nuclear disarmament. It would do so against the advice of its leadership and despite the determined campaign of its leader. But it would do so nevertheless. The crisis came, but with it came catharsis. The unilateralists had their day. But Hugh Gaitskell, standing on the platform of the Spa's Grand Hall, was able to end the debate on a note of hope as well as defiance:

. . . we may lose the vote today and the result may deal this Party a grave blow. It may not be possible to prevent it, but I think that there are many of us who will not accept that this blow need be mortal, who will not believe that such an end is inevitable. There are some of us who will fight and fight and fight again to save the Party we love. We will fight and fight and fight again to bring back sanity and honesty and dignity, so that our Party with its great past may retain its glory and greatness.

Twice he used the phrase, each "fight" emphasised more than the last, each "fight" a little louder than the one before. When he sat down, I knew that even if the Spa was blown or washed away there were some things that the landslide could not engulf.

Of course the Spa remains. It stood in unexpected fair weather three years almost to the day after the great nuclear debate. By then, the fortunes of the Labour Party had changed. It had transcended the upheavals of 1959 and 1960. It had survived Hugh Gaitskell's death. It returned to Scarborough confident of imminent election victory, certain that it had a distinctive role to play in shaping a new Britain that could face the demands of a more complicated age. Sitting in the huge dining-room of the Grand Hotel, looking out over Scarborough and the sea, I felt no doubts about the Labour Party's future.

That dining-room was, perhaps, a place from which to look back rather than forward. Time, and a hundred salesmen's conventions, have left their mark on the Grand Hotel. Once it was the summer aspiration of all Yorkshire middle classes. Indeed, on its opening day in the summer of 1867 it claimed to be the handsomest hotel in Europe. It was certainly one of the most modern—with Haden's Patent Warming Apparatus, and speaking tubes linking every floor to the servants' quarters—and probably one of the largest, with a bedroom for every day of the year. Ninety-six years later it had turned seedy, but the view it offered of Scarborough on an autumn afternoon was idyllic. Below to the left, the town's slightly embarrassed amusement arcade was just visible—buried within it the remains of a sixteenth-century manor house which serves beneath its moulded ceilings the viands of "King Richard III's Cake and Steak House". The ruined castle stood out sharp on its hill and the little lighthouse gleamed white on its jetty. Below them the sea sparkled as sea should and the boats bobbed in the harbour in the way romantic boats are supposed to bob. In the curve of the South Bay, the Spa was actually bathed in sunlight.

The morning—the morning of October 1st—had belonged to Harold Wilson. He had spoken on "Labour and the Scientific Revolution"—

perhaps not the most propitious subject for those who want a little poetry in their politics. But in that, as in so much else, he had caught the mood of Britain.

At the very time that even the MCC has abolished the distinction between amateurs and professionals, in science and industry we are content to remain a nation of Gentlemen in a world of Players.

Harold Wilson spoke for the professionals and promised them that the new Britain would be "forged in the white heat of technological revolution". It seemed the beginning of the brave new world—not Aldous Huxley's but Miranda's. If the Spa was washed away, we would build a new one. If the cliff seemed likely to crumble, we would hold it up. If the sea threatened to wash us all away, we would simply turn it back.

A BACKWARD GLANCE

SOUTH OF THE Humber, all the way through Lincolnshire and on into Suffolk and Norfolk, many of the market towns and most of the market villages have great mediaeval churches pointing perpendicular to heaven from the prosperous plains of wheat and barley. The bigger towns have county council offices and regimental depots. Their solicitors wear tweed suits both for court and for conveyancing. Their publicans are retired Wing Commanders with cars modified to carry large dogs or pull small horse-boxes. They are comfortable and certain places. And around every corner there are relics of the lost civilisation which inhabited the towns of rural England, when cars were scarce, day trippers rare and coffee bars yet to be invented.

Beverley is just like that. It has deep old-fashioned greengroceries with brass weighing-scales in their furthest recesses. It has garages where pre-war petrol pumps, with heads, necks and shoulders, stand under glass and wrought-iron canopies designed to protect Lanchesters from the east coast drizzle. It was the capital of the East Riding and the home of the East Yorkshire Regiment. It has shops whose names evoke past glories like battle honours—Akrill and Sons, Gunmakers; Pottage Brothers, Hardware. In fact, it might have been picked up in Lincolnshire, carried north and set down on the Yorkshire side of the Humber. That is save for only one thing. In most of the wool and wheat towns of East Anglia there is a splendid church. Beverley, the wool and wheat town of the Holderness Plain, has two; both big enough to be cathedrals in ordinary counties and each beautiful enough to ensure that for seven hundred years they have lived in competitive glory.

"Unlike the Minster," the *Plan and Brief Notes* of St Mary's Church begins, "this church owes its great architectural interest to having been developed through four hundred years of almost continuous building." The *Guide* is only slightly less subtle in its faint praise. "Lovely St Mary's, unequalled in all England," is quoted as the considered judgement of the late Sir Tatton Sykes, a figure in architectural criticism whose importance rests solely on his perception that St Mary's was the best, not the second best, of English churches. At the other end of the town, the Minster is majestically patronising. "It is remarkable," its guide begins, "that so

small a town ... should have two such large and graceful churches."
The real message comes a sentence later. "It is significant of their genuine
beauty and dignity that some visitors have been full of praise for the
Minster after visiting St Mary's (and mistaking it for the minster!) and
have been astounded later when confronted with the larger and more
stately church at the end of a few minutes' walk."

In fact, the existence of two such churches in Beverley is wholly un-
remarkable. At the end of the fifteenth century, Beverley was the second
great city of the north and one of the ten great towns of England. At one
end was the Minster, the Collegiate Church, near to the Monastic House
founded by Bishop John of York who became Saint John of Beverley.
That was the church's church, the place where priests were prepared for
prayer and proselytising. At the other end of the town, St Mary's was
built as the church of the people—at least, of the people substantial enough
in mediaeval England to become members of one of Beverley's thirty-
eight craft guilds.

The Minster is the great "English" church of northern England. Its
west front, tower and porch are Perpendicular English. Its choir and
transept are Early English. Its nave is Decorated English. Its Norman font
is palpably French, but five hundred years after it was set in place it was
provided with a wholly English Georgian cover. The oak organ screen is
pure Gilbert Scott and, therefore, pure nineteenth-century English.
Amongst the saints and martyrs who enliven and ennoble its niches are
figures who, although uncanonised, are wholly English, Queen Victoria
and her son Edward VII.

St Mary's can certainly rival the Minster in royal anachronisms. In
1445, the twenty-third year of the reign of Henry IV, the chancel ceiling
was adorned with his portrait and that of all those kings who were known
or believed to have preceded him. The ceiling was restored in 1863 and
completely repainted in 1939. On the eve of the Second World War,
overcome by love and loyalty, the Parish Council decreed that the
likeness of the legendary Lucrine be obliterated and replaced by the head
and shoulders of George VI. He still smiles down on the choir, a modern
joker amongst the medieval playing cards. If that square yard of ceiling is
a blemish on St Mary's beauty, it is the only one.

The great west front of St Mary's is probably the finest church façade
in England. It was the model and inspiration for the bigger (though
certainly not better) gable end to King's College Chapel, plagiarised in
Cambridge eighty years later. The great central tower stands today
exactly as its mediaeval designers intended. To the credit of early English

architects, their vision often exceeded their capabilities. Too often the reach of their imagination exceeded the grasp of their builders. Steeples toppled over and walls caved in, and during the years spent raising the money to build them up again the fashion in English architecture changed and pieces were put together in an alien style. True to the tradition of excessive aspiration, on April 29th, 1520, St Mary's central tower collapsed on to the nave. Men, women and children at Sunday service went quickly to heaven or slowly into crippled middle age. The burghers of Beverley found the money to replace the tower at once. Within four years, it was rebuilt. Despite the "five hundred years of continuous building", St Mary's remains as God and the masons of the middle ages intended it. It has been surrounded and hemmed in by the bustling life of busy Beverley. It is difficult to step back and enjoy its full glory, impossible to see the west porch uncluttered by parked cars and lamp standards. But if there was nothing else in Beverley, St Mary's would make it stand out from other market towns. But there is something else. Half a mile away is the "larger and more stately" Minster.

St Mary's and the Minster are the two great marks of Beverley's mediaeval pre-eminence. But four hundred years after Hull had overtaken it in size and significance the capital of the East Riding made its indelible mark on English life and literature. Thomas Scragg invented his clay-pipe-making machine in Beverley and, at a single prosaic stroke, revolutionised British agriculture. After 1845, men who owned half a herd or rented half an acre could afford to drain their land as the fields were drained on the great improving farms of East Anglia and the Home Counties. Scragg is largely forgotten in Britain and wholly unremembered in Beverley. But he enabled a million cows to walk on what used to be water. It was a miracle of sorts and it helped to feed the multitudes of the industrial revolution.

Two decades after Scragg had set his complicated wheels in motion, Anthony Trollope, in his own words, "persisted in going to Beverley". At the age of 62, having failed to become the Parliamentary Candidate for a safe seat in Essex and possessing "an almost insane desire" to sit in the House of Commons, he offered himself to the town's 12,000 inhabitants and 2,500 electors. The campaign turned out to be "the most wretched fortnight of my manhood".

I was subject to bitter tyranny from grinding vulgar tyrants. . . . From morning to evening every day I was taken round the lanes and bye-ways of that uninteresting town. . . . Perhaps my strongest sense of dis-

"Goodbye to Yorkshire"

"Wish You Were Here"

"They Also Serve"

"The Name on the Knife Blade"

"Limestone Country"

"Out of Season"

"Heart and Homeland"

"The Halfway Place"

comfort arose from the conviction that my political ideas were all leather and prunella to the men whose votes I was soliciting. They cared nothing for my doctrine and could not even be made to understand that they should try.

Yet worse was to come:

It had come to pass that political cleanliness was odious to the citizen. There was something grand in the scorn with which a leading Liberal turned up his nose at me when I told him that there should be no bribery, no treating, not even a pint of beer on our side! What a matter of study to perceive how at Beverley politics were appreciated because they might subserve electoral purposes and how little it was understood that electoral purposes, which are themselves a nuisance, should be endured in order that they may subserve politics.

Of course Anthony Trollope was beaten by the sitting Tory Member, Sir Henry Edwards, Chairman of the Beverley Waggon Company. Trollope petitioned against the result, following a familiar path trodden by his Liberal predecessors in 1837, 1857 and 1859. In the High Court a hundred citizens were found guilty of corruption. According to the Royal Commission that followed a year later, of the 1010 electors who voted, only seventy-eight were not bribed. The town was disenfranchised and Trollope's hopes of "doing the grandest work that a man may do" were over for ever.

Trollope deserves little sympathy. He had been warned of the outcome by a local political panjandrum whose prediction proved unreasonably correct. "You will spend a thousand pounds and lose the election. You will petition and lose a thousand pounds. There will be a commission and the borough will be disenfranchised." But his undying obsession with politics and Parliament drove him into the hopeless contest. The bitterness of the inevitable defeat provoked attacks on the borough which were as unattractive as they were unjust.

Victorian Beverley was not an "uninteresting town". To the north, the town proper began with the North Bar and its gateway, restored in 1409 for £96. 9. $11\frac{1}{2}$. The gate still stands, too ancient to demolish and so low and narrow that the double-decker buses of the East Yorkshire Traction Company are designed with concave corners to their roofs. Outside what was the wall is the Westwood, the common land where freemen can still graze their sheep and cattle. Since Trollope's time it has deteriorated. It is now hemmed in with stout Edwardian houses and its open sweep is marred and mottled by the stands and paddocks of Beverley racecourse. But inside the gate, North Bar Within begins with a line of classic Georgian houses, leading south past St Mary's and the Market Cross to the Minster. It is a road Trollope should have loved to canvass. In fact, he hated every step he took. His hatred is recorded in a dozen political novels.

In *Phineas Redux*, the pressures put upon Phineas Finn during the Tarkenville By-Election were the sort of pressures Trollope resisted and resented in Beverley.

> Mr Ruddles was a Dissenter, but the very strong opinion which Mr Ruddles now expressed as to the necessity that the new candidate should take up the Church question did not spring at all from his own religious conviction. His present duty called upon him, if possible, to have a Liberal candidate returned for the borough with which he was connected, and not to disseminate the doctrines of his own seat. . . .

Mr Trigger, the Conservative Agent in *Ralph the Heir*, no doubt shared many characteristics with the draper who fought, bribed and won in the Conservative interest at Beverley in 1868, but the election ethics that he practised were not unlike those thrust on Trollope by his Liberal sponsors in the same campaign.

> The idea of purity of elections . . . made him feel very sick. It was an idea which he hated with his whole heart. There was to him something absolutely mean and ignoble in the idea of a man coming forward to represent a borough in Parliament without paying regular fees. . . .

Because of his failure at Beverley, Trollope came to abominate the town as Mr Trigger abominated political purity. Beverley hardly noticed. A town in which the residential saint has raised the dead in the public market place can transcend the pique of a travelling novelist turned unsuccessful politician. God set Beverley in good soil. And the soil produced centuries of certain success for the whole of Holderness, and even today Beverley continues as the centre of a serene and secure part of Yorkshire, a confident East Riding sun surrounded by a galaxy of self-satisfied villages.

The Georgian-type semi-detached dwellings at Cherry Burton would be at home in the soft south. If Cherry Burton did not exist, it would be necessary for Wates or Wimpeys to create it. Bishop Burton, with its crescent-shaped pond surrounded by white fences and whiter houses, has the more permanent sort of confidence that comes from half a century of no change greater than a new war memorial and an annual coat of lime-wash. It is calm and courteous and offers its visitors a consciously friendly invitation: "Please help to feed the ducks." At first it seems there are no ducks to be fed. But as soon as bread hits water, the whole armada sets sail from underneath the overhanging trees. The visitor ought not to be surprised. If there had been no ducks to feed, Bishop Burton would not have given false hope. East Yorkshire's signposts are gracious, not deceptive. Between Beverley and the sea, the stranger is chivalrously saved from disappointment and a wasted journey: "Ulrone Village; no seaside."

The stranger is also prevented from intruding into the comfortable world of the Holderness Plain and breaking the ancient calm of its pastoral prosperity which has hardly changed in five hundred years. Of course, Holderness is no longer the land of the Halifaxes and the Hothams. It is no more the exclusive preserve of the seventeenth-century aristocracy than Beverley is the Beaver fields on which the churches were built and to which the merchants came to market. Time and progress have brought the commuter, the speculative builder, the week-end cottage, the fertiliser factory and the battery hen. But it is still a different sort of Yorkshire: flat rather than rugged, arable rather than industrial, historically prosperous rather than traditionally poor, the place where the East Riding turns into East Anglia. And the signposts and sentinels which mark the frontier are the Minster and St Mary's. For those who give a backward glance before they go on south, Yorkshire could hardly provide a better memory.

FOUR

Pleasant Pastures

———————————

HEART AND HOMELAND

THE WHARFE IS a particularly and peculiarly Yorkshire river. It is neither the longest nor the widest river in the county. Formal pride of place must go to the Ouse, the real source of the Humber, part of the road that kept the imperial connection between Rome and Eboracum, and the route by which the message was sent home that Constantine's legionaries had proclaimed him Emperor in York. In the far north, Middlesbrough was built to be the great port of the Tees. In the east, Hull exists because of the Humber, and in the south, at Sheffield, five separate streams drove Sheffield's water-wheels and turned its grindstones. A dozen rivers rise in the Pennines. One turns treacherously west and runs through Lancashire to the sea. The rest stay true to Yorkshire, rush out of the hills and curl their way through the Dales. But none is quite so wholly Yorkshire as the Wharfe. Say "river" and "Yorkshire" in a single sentence and only one name immediately comes to mind. If the Nile is the mother of Egypt, the Wharfe is Yorkshire's mam.

The Wharfe rises at the highest point of the West Riding, between Whernside and Pen-y-Ghent. When it reaches Bolton it is still not sure if it is an infant stream rushing forward into the future, or an elderly river dawdling its way towards the inevitable end. Through the grounds of Bolton Abbey it meanders so wide and shallow that children tiptoe across its stepping stones. A half mile up the dale it races through the narrow Strid as fast and as deep as any river in the country. It flows through Tadcaster and into its breweries. It runs past Wetherby and its racecourse. And on its bank stand Ilkley and Otley, the two most Yorkshire towns in all of Yorkshire.

Of course, part of Ilkley's fame springs from its moor, Mary-Jane and her bare-headed sweetheart, his predictable illness, prognosticated death and gothic burial. But there is much more to Ilkley than that. Once it was a Victorian spa, a holiday resort for the prosperous burghers at Bradford and Leeds. All the way up the hill to the Cow and Calf Rocks (which are remarkably unlike any animal domesticated or wild) the great grey stone hotels are a reminder of a previous prosperity. The Stoney Lea and the Craiglands are clearly places where once the Yorkshire pudding was light and the after-dinner conversation heavy. No doubt

the Yorkshire pudding has survived, but much has changed since the
wool merchants and cloth-makers arrived at the fine Victorian station
and were welcomed by the prospect of the fine Victorian Spa Hall. The
Cow and Calf Hotel (in the lee and shadow of the bovine rocks) is solid
and timelessly dependable. But it has clearly capitulated to part of the
twentieth century. It has a *Beergarden* and *Samantha's Discotheque*, where
Yorkshire respectability is commemorated in the immortal warning: "The
management reserves the right to refuse admission to anyone who is
untidily dressed."

From the top of the Cow and Calf Rocks and the extremity of the
Cow and Calf car park, all of Wharfedale stretches out towards Wetherby
and the Ouse. The houses in Ilkley are dark grey, like proper Yorkshire
houses, with only the occasional red-brick villa to disturb the solid
certainty of almost constant stone. On the northern slope of the dale, a
few white houses stand out against the khaki hillside. The soil looks rich
enough to provide both pleasure and profit, but only after hard graft and
careful husbandry. Those are the qualities in which the dalesmen excel.
So the farms of Wharfedale have the look of comfortable contentment
that comes from a history of always doing a little better than only making
ends meet.

Just in view, around an elbow in the hills, is Denton Hall. Thomas
Fairfax was born in the first house on that site. Captain of the Yorkshire
Puritans, victorious General in the Parliamentary cause at Naseby and
Marston Moor, he won and held half of his native county for Cromwell
and the Commonwealth and went on to be Commander in Chief of the
whole Ironside army. He possessed most of the qualities which Yorkshiremen admire. He was sober, pious, industrious, shrewd and brave. He had
the habit of winning. At Marston Moor, as Lieutenant General of Horse
under his father's overall command, he fought his wounded way from
one flank of the battle to the other, joined forces with Cromwell's
dragoons and commanded the united cavalry charge which won the day.
But despite his virtues, his victories and his valour, he never developed
an intolerable excess of prejudice or principle. He was wholly opposed to
the death of Charles I. Convinced the trial was simply meant to be the
formal prelude to a pre-determined execution, he refused to sit in judgement on the King. At the opening of the Commission that passed for judge
and jury, Lady Fairfax in the gallery left no doubt about her husband's
absence and attitude. "The Lord Fairfax is not there in person. He will
never sit amongst them and they do him wrong to name him a
Commissioner."

With the Lord Protector dead, the Commonwealth in confusion and the realm at risk, Fairfax was one of the pragmatic Puritans who chose a return of the Stuarts rather than the risk of chaos and anarchy. He was amongst the conspirators who determined to restore the monarchy and led the five emissaries who sailed to Breda, accepted the King's promise of a general pardon for old enemies and support for the Anglican church, then offered him the crown of England. It turned out to be a most reasonable revolution. The plot was laid and executed in a practical Yorkshire fashion at Nun Appleton Hall which stands where the Wharfe and Ouse combine.

There is hardly a passage or period in Yorkshire life and work that is not commemorated somewhere along the Wharfe. Thomas Chippendale was born in Otley. His father was the village joiner and part of a line of carpenters so long that the sentimental have assumed that the family were given a name which combined their trade and the part of Yorkshire in which it was practised. The sentimentalists are wrong. Chippendale proclaims origin, but it does not denote occupation. It was originally the name of a place not a man—and a place, it has to be admitted, in Lancashire. The word "chip" (used to describe either a fragment of wood or the process by which it is flaked away) was unknown in England until the fourteenth century. Yet Chippendale in Lancashire—the "shopping place" and market town—appears in the Domesday Book of 1086. There can be little doubt that the family took its name from the town and that the Chippendales originated on the wrong side of the Pennines. But they had the good sense to move east. That at least is cause for rejoicing.

Thomas Chippendale made his fortune and reputation in London, but the dales are full of his work. The eighteenth century was an era of great house building in Yorkshire. From Vanbrugh's "town and fortified city" at Castle Howard to beautiful Harewood House, Chippendale's furniture graced every room.

The houses that line the road from Otley and Ilkley are of a more modest order, but they are equally part of Yorkshire history. They range from the Burley Hall Hotel (a model of Georgian restraint, and proof that in Yorkshire, Regency art and elegance was not confined to the castles and mansions) to the pine and stucco bungalows of the sixties' building boom. Aesthetically and geographically in between are the long black houses mortgaged to wool and worsted in the nineteenth century. Some are so dark and heavy that they could easily be called Wildfell Hall or Thrushcroft Grange. From their windows the householders of the Ilkley-to-Otley road can see Wharfedale from its narrow beginning high in the fells to its end in the open fields of Knaresborough Forest. And a few have at the bottom of their gardens what Wordsworth called "the stately river Wharfe".

In Otley at Christmas 1884, looking out across that river, John Ruskin saw "the perfect Turner painting". Ruskin and the Pre-Raphaelites were properly addicted to Yorkshire. Ruskin himself lived briefly in Sheffield and Lizzie Siddall almost bankrupted the entire Brotherhood by insisting on spending a holiday in that city.

But Ruskin's judgement on the Yorkshire landscape was more than the product of sentiment. The river shone in the winter sunlight. In the fields on the far bank pale green merged into pale brown. Above them the hills were purple and slate grey. And almost out of sight, the arches of the old stone bridge joined town and country. The Wharfe at Otley was the sort of picture Turner used to paint and Turner had crossed its bridge a thousand times. For Otley became the base from which he sallied forth to capture Yorkshire.

In two hundred years the bridge itself has hardly changed. A special causeway has been constructed to separate pedestrians from traffic and it is now possible to cross in single safety if not double comfort. But the arches stand with a timeless determination that has not altered since 1775. Nobody knows when the first bridge was built across the Wharfe at Otley. For hundreds of years, successive bridges were built and quickly washed away. Wharfe was the Saxon river Guerf, called "swift" because one winter out of every five it turned into a torrent. In 1675, reliable piers were sunk into the river bed. They lasted for exactly one hundred years. Then there was "the terrible storm of wind and rain, which lasted for thirty-six hours and part of the bridge was blown down". A year later it was restored, widened and strengthened to proportions of such solidarity that it could clearly stand for another dozen centuries.

Today the bridge looks so permanent and the river appears so peaceful that it is difficult to believe in a flood that might sweep it aside. Despite the marked and numbered poles which stand in the clean clear water as a warning that the rainbow's promise does not apply to rivers, the Wharfe at Otley is a reassuring river. Each side of the bridge, there are lawns and flowers and benches. On the north bank a row of Dickensian cottages faces out across the strand. Ducks bob and swans glide. Turner knew a good view when he saw one—which is why he stayed so often in Otley.

At least, it is one of the reasons. In 1798, J. M. W. Turner made his first visit to Yorkshire in search of the Abbey ruins which have fascinated painters since the Reformation. During his northern tour he met Doctor

Thomas Durham Whitaker, the author and publisher of local histories. Turner agreed to illustrate *The Parish of Whalley*. His engravings included Farnley Hall in Otley. Walter Fawkes, the squire of Farnley, was enthralled by both the painting and its painter. He became Turner's friend and patron. For twenty-five years, a Christmas package of game and goose pie followed Turner to wherever he was painting. In 1851, it was ready for collection at Otley station when the news of Turner's death arrived at Farnley Hall.

In the fifty years of their friendship, Turner was a constant visitor to Farnley Hall. It was the base from which he made expeditions north to Richmond to work with Whitaker on *The History of Richmondshire* and the home to which he returned with his fifty sketches of the Rhine. It was to Fawkes that Turner gave *The Dortrecht Packet Boat Becalmed* and from the Squire's house he set off to paint *Kirkstall Abbey*. By the time the friendship was ended by Turner's death, Farnley Hall was stuffed with his work. So many Turner paintings hung on the Fawkes family walls that when Ruskin visited Otley, he took one to bed with him each night to study its individual beauty in silent isolation.

For all of the nineteenth century Otley was the archetypal West Riding town, a microcosm of Victorian Yorkshire, embodying in its life and work the painful progress that was being enjoyed or endured throughout the county. The railway arrived in 1850, but only after it had cost the lives of twenty-three men killed whilst digging Bramhope Tunnel. A local tanner's son discharged his father's bankruptcy, became Mayor of Leeds, was elected to Parliament, served as Secretary of State for Ireland, was raised to the peerage, was appointed Chairman of the Great Northern Railway Company, and—glory above all other glories—his son, the Honourable F. S. Jackson, played cricket for Yorkshire and England.

Ten years before William Jackson, First Baron Allerton, went to the Irish Office the waves of Fenian outrage had flowed along the Wharfe. The movement from the sacred to the profane begun with the Dissolution of the Monasteries had been completed at Bolton by the conversion of the Priory Gatehouse into the Duke of Devonshire's shooting box. His son, Lord Frederick Cavendish, was appointed Lord Lieutenant of Ireland. It was a brief obligation. On the day of his arrival in Dublin, he was murdered in Phoenix Park. In Bolton Abbey's grounds a memorial was erected and on it was engraved Mr Gladstone's perfect tribute—"full of love for that country, full of hope for her future, full of capacity to render her service". To Gladstone the death of his protégé was forever an "unhealed wound". To Mr W. E. Forster, Irish Secretary and Member of Parliament for Bradford, it was more evidence of the need to move from conciliation to coercion. The people along the banks of the Wharfe responded calmly. John Morley recorded their reaction.

An appeal confronted the electors of the North West Riding as they went to the polls a few days later. "Vote for Gaythorne Hardy and avenge the death of Lord Frederick Cavendish." They responded by placing Gaythorne Hardy's opponent at the head of the poll by a majority of 2000.

It was the reaction to be expected from Victorian Yorkshire. Ireland was a distant alien place. The passing of Lord Frederick was to be regretted and mourned. But his death did not justify the abandonment of old loyalties or the mindless neglect of other problems nearer home.

At home in Otley, the nineteenth century had produced all the works and wonders that had been expected at its dawn. As the old leather trade declined and Otley determined to live less and less on its market, the town enjoyed one of the mechanical miracles that were supposed to characterise the industrial revolution. Otley's era of invention came late and it took time. During the three years that followed 1858, David Payne and William Dawson developed a new sort of printing press. The "Wharfedale" put Otley at the centre of the northern printing industry and provided the town with the men and money to pursue the pastimes of Victorian Yorkshire.

The Chapels flourished, the Brass Band Movement (including William Dawson, cornetist and conductor as well as inventor) prospered. The Mechanics' Institute (first President William Ackroyd, whose Worsted Spinning Mill is still in business) grew year by year. There was nothing that happened in Yorkshire that did not happen in Otley. It stood, the wholly Yorkshire town, on the banks of the wholly Yorkshire river. It does not look like the capital of its region or even the county town of its Riding. But it does look the heart and homeland of Yorkshire. It could hardly have a more noble title.

THE HALFWAY PLACE

Harrogate and its people go well together. The town possesses all the attributes of the determined middle-aged ladies who frequent its teashops and patronise its not-quite-chic boutiques. It is moderately well preserved. It is deeply conscious of the need to keep up appearances and remain, at least in public, neat and tidy. It is insulated from the uglier aspects of life in the West Riding. And, above all, it is self-satisfied.

It has a lot to be satisfied about. On a bright May morning with the sun shining on the carefully manicured gardens of the Royal and Montpelier Parades, it is easy to believe that respectability was invented in Harrogate. The tulips bloom clean and upright. The grass on the Stray is crisp and perfect. Old gentlemen with their dogs and young boys with their footballs leave no marks on its smooth green surface. Rough brown patches may appear on common common-land but the Stray is too well-disciplined and self-possessed to allow it to happen there. Inevitably, with its sprinkling of Georgian houses approached over the green open land, Harrogate is compared by superficial southerners to Blackheath. The comparison is absurd. Wat Tyler would not have dared to assemble his Peasants' Revolt on the Stray. The Stray has its own, highly appropriate, place in English history. There, on a summer Sunday in 1876, Bishop Bickersteth wrote *Peace, Perfect Peace*.

No doubt that is what the commuting executives of Leeds and Bradford still hope to find in Harrogate; and no doubt, more often than not, their hopes are gratified. For despite all its advantages as a holiday resort and its undoubted success as a conference centre it seems to attract only the most sober of visitors. Some seem to have been born sober. Others have either achieved it or had it thrust upon them by Harrogate's all-pervasive propriety. However the characteristic is acquired, there is no doubt that most of the visitors to the Old Swan, the Granby and the Majestic—both the proud parents up for the half-term liberation at Harrogate Ladies College and the local-government officials in corporate consultation about the salaries of sewage inspectors—instinctively identify with the card they place outside their bedroom doors. It ought to be the motto of the town. Do not disturb.

In Harrogate it has always been like that. Although a Spa, it was too far north to attract the regular trade of Tudor and Stuart hypochondriacs. Even in Hanoverian England, when the obsession with polluted water was at its height, Harrogate was still well out of the main mineral stream. Tom Fashion would not have made the trip to Harrogate, even for a wedding. And the non-fictional wits and bucks of the period—most notably Sydney Smith—heaped Harrogate with their abuse. Their prejudice was against the northern situation rather than the services it could provide. As a Spa it had no equal. Eighty-eight separate mineral springs gushed forth health and vitality within a mile of the town centre. The water came in four different varieties. From the Royal Pump Room and the Sulphur Well beneath it issues the most famous and the foulest of them all.

Below the Royal Pump Room bubbles a "strong sulphur" well. Strong it certainly is; strong enough to be smelled a hundred yards away across the road in Valley Gardens and strong enough to descend on visitors to the Pump Room Museum like a thick sulphur poultice. Only visitors with the least sensitive of nostrils can concentrate on the collection of Victorian un-memorabilia or genuinely focus their attention on the faded pictures in the creaking biographs. Being Yorkshire, a virtue was made out of the peculiar nausea that the smell induced. Not only was its particular unpleasantness a sure sign of its medical efficacy, it was a proper subject for the self-deprecating jokes with which Yorkshiremen obscure their faults.

> As Satan was flying o'er Harrogate well
> His senses were charmed with the heat and the smell

was engraved on the Royal Pump Room frieze, and apparently attracted rather than deterred custom. The frieze is gone, but the sulphur well remains. Above it is the Royal Pump Room Museum of Local Antiquities, built during 1846 in the heavy Victorian style that characterises Harrogate in the way Regency elegance typifies other, more fashionable, spas. The style persists throughout the town, in the Royal Hall, in the Assembly Rooms, in the Royal Bath Hospital and in half the town's hotels and shops. Sometimes the hotels are enlivened by a Georgian colonnade or decorated with a wrought-iron canopy. But basically the town is uncertain Victorian —hovering uneasily between grace and practicality, a halfway place between classes of English society and periods of English history.

Indeed, natives of Harrogate regard its status as a halfway place as one of its principal claims to fame. It stands, all the guidebooks proclaim, halfway between the capitals of England and Scotland. From the top of the observatory tower on its Harlow Hill, the Tees, the Humber and Morecambe Bay are all in view. No battles have actually been fought in or from Harrogate, but it is *near* to Stamford Bridge where King Harold and his housecarls defeated the Vikings of Harold Hardrada; *close* to Northallerton, where Stephen's English Knights beat the invading clansmen at the battle of the Standard; *hard by* Towton, where Edward IV won the crown of England in a blinding snowstorm, and *within reach* of Marston Moor, where Sir Thomas Fairfax and his Yorkshire Puritans defeated Prince Rupert of the Rhine and made all Yorkshire safe for Commonwealth and Parliament.

Harrogate is the Yorkshire town where nothing happened. But five miles to the north-east, Knaresborough has enough history for both places. The semi-detached suburbia of one passes imperceptibly into the residential bungalows of the other, with only the boroughs' coats of arms to mask the boundaries in between. But once into Knaresborough the difference is obvious and profound. From the first sight of the Railway Bridge across the River Nidd—part of the industrial revolution's tribute to Roman civilisation—it is clear that things have happened in Knaresborough.

The town and its castle had their great period of regal glory during the reign of the first four Edwards. Edward I gave the castle to Queen Eleanor. Piers Gaveston held it for Edward II against the northern barons. Edward III gave the castle, the town and the Forest of Knaresborough to Queen Philippa as part of her dowry. And long before the king's favourite men and mistresses inhabited the castle, it had played its part in English history. Hugh de Morville was once its master, and it was to Knaresborough he returned for rest and refuge with Reginald FitzUrse, William de Traci and Richard Brito after the four knights had murdered Thomas à Becket in Canterbury Cathedral on Christmas Day 1170.

At least according to T. S. Eliot, Hugh de Morville was a particularly Yorkshire regicide. "You are," he tells the audience ingratiatingly, "hard-headed, sensible people . . . not to be taken in by emotional clap-trap." St Thomas's life and death, the guilt of his assassins and the consequences of his martyrdom, all have to be "considered soberly".

The castle, like all good Yorkshire castles, was demolished by Oliver Cromwell and his New Model Army. It now stands a bleak, black ruin surrounded by neat green gardens, a marvellous vantage point from which to see the terraced town and watch the Nidd swing south under the Railway Bridge. On a sunny day, it is a happy castle, guarding a happy town and river—a castle with a moat turned into a children's playground;

a town where tiny houses climb up the valley side; a river speckled with hired rowing boats and fibre-glass canoes.

Yet the town had an unhappy history even before the Roundheads knocked the castle about a bit. Richard II spent desperate months there, before his final journey to Pontefract. Oliver Cromwell mourned there the death of his son, killed in the skirmishing that accompanied Marston Moor. Sir Henry Slingsby, who fought for Charles Stuart, was beheaded there and his decapitated body lies in the parish church. In the church, in the town, in the country beyond, the Slingsbys are everywhere, though the line is now extinct. It ended with the death of Sir Charles Slingsby, drowned crossing the Nidd in the best traditions of a family which made a practice of losing its scions in the local river.

The Slingsbys represent the old aristocracy of Yorkshire. To the south (near enough to Harrogate for that town to take a vicarious pleasure in its proximity) a newer Yorkshire aristocracy has opened Harewood House to the paying public. It is not simply the Presidency of Leeds United or control of the National Opera that makes the Lascelles family part of a different generation. Francis Slingsby fought for Queen Elizabeth two hundred years before Henry Lascelles, a Northallerton squire, bought Gawthorp Hall. In its grounds his son built Harewood House.

The north front of Harewood House is probably the most elegant prospect in Yorkshire. Its clean stone is matched by its clean lines, a triumph for geometrical balance and the virtues of architectural restraint. The house's basic design was by John Carr, a practical architect from York, but before the first stone was laid, Robert Adam had arrived in Harewood village to advise on how the church could be restored. From then on the building of Harewood House was an uneasy partnership between the unknown Yorkshireman and the fashionable Scot. Only the entrance hall remains true to Carr's first design, yet what they produced betrays no marks of dispute or disharmony. The exterior of Harewood House is as serene as it is beautiful.

The inside is like a catalogue to the treasures of English domestic architecture—beautiful but hardly serene. It bulges with furniture made by a local carpenter who—having left Otley and found fame in London society—gladly accepted commissions from his old county. What Chippendale made (sometimes wood painted to look like gold, sometimes mahogany carved consistently with Adam's classical design) had to be augmented and enhanced by later squires turned gentry. A hundred years after the house was finished, Charles Barry was asked to improve it. It is a tribute to his genius that he changed so much but spoilt so little.

Some parts of the house are actually better for his renovation. The great concave bookcase, curving across the Spanish library, its rigid vertical lines picked out in strips of brass, is literally too good to look true. With its leather-and-gilt books in precise rows along its perfectly proportioned shelves it produces *trompe l'œil* in reverse—the illusion of a complicated Hollywood backcloth painted with sumptuous precision to show how English gentlemen once kept their books.

Very few English gentlemen kept their books beneath ceilings like Harewood ceilings. Harewood House has everything. So as well as Capability Brown outside it has Angelica Kaufman *and* Adam overhead. No doubt the ceilings are rare and wonderful, incorporating all the plaques and meander patterns of ancient Greece with all the colours that ever appeared in a Neapolitan ice. Undoubtedly they are part of Robert Adam's great design. But on the elegant lily of Harewood House they are one drop of gilt too much.

That is an unusual allegation to level at anything within the hinterland of which Harrogate is so proud. For Harrogate is compact country. Its virtues are discipline and good order, neatness and sobriety. The attributes are typified in the tiny terraced houses of Knaresborough and the regimented roses on the Stray. Splendour is not its style. Its instincts are to understate rather than over-emphasise. Harewood House, ceilings and all, stands out as a magnificent exception to the reticent rule—not the sort of house on which Harrogate families would normally spend their fortunes, but certainly the sort of place they boast is only just down the road.

CHURCH TRIUMPHANT

IN ITS HEART, York is still a mediaeval city. Roman remains (still many of them waiting to be excavated from beneath the parks and pavements) prove that it flourished and prospered six hundred years before King Edwin of Northumbria built his little wooden shrine. George Hudson's railway provided a new perspective and extra dimension six hundred years after Walter de Gray began to build the great cathedral church. But when, after two centuries of holy sweat and pious blisters Neville and Thorsby completed the work de Gray began, the pattern of the years before was blotted out by a magnificent, triple-towered, cruciform shadow. For the rest of time, York was destined to shelter, in proper mediaeval style, under the protection and patronage of the Minster— sometimes the church militant, often the church triumphant, occasionally the church beleaguered, but always the church visible, inescapable in its architectural glory.

The Minster has dominated York since the days of bad King John. From time to time there have been attempts to put it in its place. Archbishop Scroop (having parleyed in nearby Gaultree Forest and unaccountably accepted the word of a Lancastrian) lost his head to prove that the Yorkshire mace and mitre were held in fief to a Welsh King. Cromwell stabled Ironsides' horses in the nave to show that even the mightiest steeple house was not safe from his destructive zeal. But the Minster survived, according to John Evelyn, "the cathedral which of all the great churches in England had been best preserved from ye furie of ye sacrilegious". And three hundred years after Cromwell was dead, buried, disinterred and hanged, another soldier—General "Stonewall" Jackson— visited York and returned to America with memories so vivid that after the battle of Richmond *The Times* reported "he spoke a few hearty words of admiration of General Robert E. Lee . . . but his most heartfelt and most enthusiastic utterances were in admiration of the Cathedral edifices of England, notably York Minster".

There was a moment when York really believed that its destiny could be changed, that it could dig up its roots from mediaeval England and plant itself at the centre of the new mechanical world. George Hudson (having met George Stevenson in Whitby, a town for which the Scottish engineer developed such an affection that he bought it and gave it to his son to represent in Parliament) devised a simple formula for making his private fortune, and his public reputation: "Mak t'railways come to York." Some rivals were bought up, others were bullied or blackguarded out of competitive existence. York became the crossroads of Victorian England. It occupied a place so centrally convenient to the new industries of the north and the midlands that for a hundred years employees and trade unionists met in the city for the highest and final stage of their ritualised arguments and formalised disagreements. A phrase has passed into the industrial lexicon as a threat and a promise: "We'll have to take it to York".

Considering itself the centre of the railway empire and the home of the Railway King, York built a railway station regally suitable to its imperial grandeur. Its cast-iron corinthian pillars (in these days of railway austerity only the half dozen near the ticket barrier are gilded, the rest are utilitarian grey) are a memorial to the belief that the permanent way was built to last. Its gothic arches are a testimony to the grandeur of the whole railway enterprise. But for permanence, power and glory the railways could hardly compete with the Minster. Even had George Hudson's empire not met the inevitable and ignominious end of companies that pay old dividends out of new investments and borrow money from their owners at inflated rates of interest, York would have remained the mediaeval city rather than the railway town.

Even had Mrs Hudson's insistence that the York–London express must not leave before her pineapple was on board not precipitated a sudden decline, the railways would not have stood a chance. They were literally over-shadowed by the Minster. Passengers by train from Durham and the north see its white magnificence through their carriage windows ten minutes before they arrive at York. Travellers by rail from Doncaster and the south get a brief glimpse of the incomparable towers standing out over the skyline of the southern city. The Minster pursues the visitors all the way into the Royal Station Hotel. From the tables of the agoraphobic dining-room visitors are distracted from their arguments about whether the pillars inside the hotel are identical to those on the station platform, and their discussions of the Dick Turpin's Bar's apparent belief that Black Beauty was a woman, by its inescapable presence. Through the windows, beyond the gardens, across the Ouse, over Lendal Bridge is the Minster. Certain and serene it smiles down on the temporary and the temporal.

Even in the Shambles, between the coy craftshops, which are separated by only the width of an Elizabethan street, its towers loom over the rooftops. And in the few places where the Minster itself is hidden, above the house-tops and around the street corners there are other churches protruding onto pavements and abutting against modern office blocks. St Mary's (with the highest spire in York), Holy Trinity (once chapel to a Benedictine priory), St Deny's and St Margaret's (both with stones which Norman masons laid) are all part of the ecclesiastical tradition of episcopal York.

In 1340, to that tradition were added the York Mystery Plays. Once they were performed by the City Guilds who pulled their pageant waggons from Toft Green to Holy Trinity and on to Jubbegate, the door of Henry Wyman, the door of Adam de la Bryg and the End of Girdle-gate. They stopped at each appointed place to perform the part of the holy story which was judged appropriate to their trade and craft. With forty-eight plays in all, every guild was able to play its own distinctive part. The Armourers portrayed the Exile from Eden. The Glovers re-enacted the Sacrifice of Cain and Abel. The Founderers and Pewterers recalled Joseph's Dream and the Mercers ended the proceedings on a note of simultaneous hope and warning with an anticipation of Judgement Day. The plays are mobile no longer. Now, every three years they are staged in the Museum Gardens, with the ruins of St Mary's Abbey as a substitute for the pageant waggons. In the years of their performance they add a special sort of visitor to those who jostle each other on York's narrow pavements every summer.

In ordinary summers half of Yorkshire seems to visit York. The parks and gardens are sprinkled with primary school pupils, their satchels and their plastic jeroboams of orangeade. The Minster is surrounded by com-plicated tripods supporting expensive cameras. The restored Merchant Taylors' Hall and the genuine fifteenth-century Hall of the Merchant Adventurers are filled with earnest amateur historians and day trippers determined to do the right thing by York and its antiquities. The narrow streets are jammed with visiting coaches and the railway station has special noticeboards demanding that specified schools congregate beneath them at specific times.

As a child, I made my first visit to York with my historically inclined father and educationally determined mother. The day was a failure. I returned home, bored and in disgrace. It was ten years before I set foot in York again. By then I was a prefect at the Sheffield City Grammar School and deeply conscious of the responsibilities such exalted rank entailed. I wanted to take the city and its churches seriously, but my concentration on things historical and spiritual was continually distracted by radios in passing cars and television sets in electrical shop windows. The young

Fred Trueman was running though the Indians at Headingley and, though my body was in York, my heart was in Leeds.

It was not even third time lucky. That was the year of the Mystery Plays and my return to the City Palatinate in the humblest capacity in all the complicated hierarchy of selective secondary education—staff husband. Ten years earlier—or thirty later—I would have enjoyed the company of twenty teenage girls. At twenty-five I found them tedious. But their conversation on the outward bus was scintillating delight compared with what was to come.

I knew that I should enjoy every episode. The Creation, the Fall and the Resurrection are all stirring stuff. I could have rejoiced at the hope of Salvation and given thanks for the promise of Life after Death. There was even a Lucifer, big and bold enough to live up to the heroic expectation that John Milton had established in my mind. But as the history of the universe yawned on in front of me, only one Christian concept was really made real—eternity. Three hours of Middle English in the Northern dialect endured on hard wooden benches creates an irresistible temptation to impious thoughts.

Down the road in Beverley, during a performance of their Mystery Plays, a little boy fell from a tree, landed on his head, died and was miraculously restored to life. John, previously Abbot of what has now become Beverley Minster, was given credit for the miracle. It helped with his canonisation, for even in Yorkshire (where it is devoutly believed that hard work and determination can achieve anything) resurrection is rare. During the second and third hours of the York performance I began to develop my own ideas of what really happened.

At first, I simply assumed that the lad had feigned death as the first strategem in a plot to have his counterfeit corpse passed over the crowd's heads in a Monte Cristo-type escape. As the evening wore on, I began to believe that, driven mad by boredom, he had cast himself suicidally down from the topmost branch—hoping that his maker would be more entertaining in fact than in fiction. Of course, the merciless church had condemned him to rise from the dead and sit out the rest of the performance.

Towards the end of the third hour I started to make silent, solemn, profane promises. If the plays ended I would lead a crusade to the Holy Land; I would make a pilgrimage to Canterbury; I would walk barefoot and penitential across the Alps to Rome. Anyway, I would go to evening service at Wadsley Church next week. It was then that out of a perfect pale blue sky the rain began to pour and the play was abandoned. I could not have been more frightened if the cherubim and the seraphim had parted the clouds to reveal an old man with a long beard and a white nightgown.

In the bus on the way home, I tried to compromise with virtue and recover lost spiritual credit by thinking beautiful thoughts about York and its magnificent Minster. I concentrated on the great East Window, according to Pugin "the most beautiful window in the world". I gave thanks that Jonathan Martin, the mad incendiarist, had been apprehended and punished. I cursed Tostig and Harold Hardrada who had sailed up the Humber with their Norwegian hordes and sacked York as a warm-up for the international with Harold of England at Stamford Bridge. I would follow the pious example of Fergus O'Connor. Imprisoned in York, awaiting trial for sedition, he persuaded the tipstaff to take him on a tour of the city. It proved uplifting. After his conviction, he sent a donation to the current Minster restoration appeal.

Restoration appeals have been a feature of York life for a hundred and fifty years, for the Minster has been in need of repair for most of its modern life. Like most of Yorkshire's ancient churches, today's Minster stands on the site of earlier edifices destroyed by time, the Viking invasion and the Norman's "harassment of the north". The Normans built their own cathedral. It was burnt down in 1137 and the remains were demolished eighty years later by Walter de Gray in preparation for the great minster he planned to build on the site of King Edwin's Chapel. He built it big as well as beautiful, so heavy that the world beneath it crumbled.

It was built of Yorkshire stone, quarried at Tadcaster and floated on rafts down the River Wharfe, borne towards York on the water that makes Tadcaster beer the best in Yorkshire. When it arrived at York, it was dragged to where the Minster was to be, along what the locals came to call Stonegate. It took twenty thousand tons of magnesian limestone to build the central tower alone. That is a lot of weight to be carried by a patch of soil—even Yorkshire soil. Yet the ground held for five hundred years and the church survived—survived even the fires of 1829 and 1840 that began the York tradition of continual restoration and constant Restoration Funds.

Although the central tower looked straight and secure, sometime during the nineteenth century it had begun to lean. At first it was almost imperceptible. Those who noticed it were accused of over-active imagination. By 1947 the evidence was too strong to refute or ignore. The scientific judgement insisted that the foundation of the central tower would not bear its hundred feet of sculptured stone much longer. And that was not all. If it collapsed, it would fall on an east wall and two west towers which were crumbling away. When the original foundations were uncovered it was judged extraordinary that the central tower had lasted a single century and wholly miraculous that it had survived for five. But providence could be trusted no longer.

Three thousand tons of concrete reinforced by two hundred tons of steel were spread under the Minster. They hardened into a new solid base on which the central tower could stand for all eternity. The tower's walls were pulled back into vertical perfection and kept straight and true by two and a half miles of metal band wound round them like binding on a splintered cricket bat. A thousand holes were drilled into the east wall and the two west towers. Each one was filled with liquid concrete that pulled the broken stones together and held them fast. The York Glaziers' Trust, who guard the Minster's glass, used the restoration scaffolding to inspect their ancient charge. The great Rose Window was completely re-leaded and its original intention was again fulfilled. The window was a celebration of the marriage of Henry VII and Elizabeth, the ancient union of the House of York and the House of Lancaster, and at every point a white and red rose was to bloom side by side. In 1486, a year after Bosworth Field, the flowers had been carefully matched. Time had destroyed a few of the couplings. In 1972 each individual floral union was restored.

That was exactly five hundred years after Archbishop Neville's service of thanksgiving that the Minster was whole and complete, and about fifteen after my mystic moment at the mystery plays. It took me about that time to recover from my one experience of divine intervention. Then, one day, walking round the restored city wall, I came to realise what York was really about. I started at Monks Bar where the ramparts lie so close to the houses of Goodram Gate and Lord Mayor's Walk that the burghers protect their rooftops with chicken wire from the teenage sentinels who patrol the battlements at night. Between the wall and the Minster were lawns and apple trees and houses; an idyll of clerical England, the hopes and dreams of ten generations of prebendaries and rural deans, a community sheltered from time and temptation by the protection and patronage of the church. It was there, on that grass between those trees in the view of those houses, that a running choirboy slipped and fell. Lying on his back he saw smoke begin to billow from under the Minster's roof.

Thanks to the early warning that his fall provided, the Minster was saved. Simple local folk called it a miracle. And why not? York is a mediaeval city and that is where miracles ought to happen. Towards the end of a Mystery Play, back in 1958, I had a little one of my own.

WORK AND WORSHIP

EAST OF THE road that runs from Harrogate to Ripon, agricultural Yorkshire rolls and ripples its way past York and Malton to the sea. In some parts of the county, the horizon is sharp and clear, a precise line drawn by factory roofs and limestone escarpments. But here the fields run endlessly on until soil and sky can no longer be distinguished. In the Pennines, farming is little more than the ownership of dishevelled sheep and the constant reconstruction of dry stone walls. But here, sleek cows graze in meadows separated by hawthorn hedges and exude all the contented confidence of a thousand years of pastoral prosperity.

The view across the Swale and over the Howardian Hills is only a glimpse of the rich farm land that covers half of Yorkshire. For Yorkshire is a rural county. The factory towns of the south-west and the barren hills that mark the border with Lancashire are the Yorkshire of the music-hall comedian and the north country comedy. But they cover only a few of the broad acres. South of Middlesbrough there is no industry in the North Riding. North of Hull, the East Riding is exclusively agricultural. Certainly the north York moors grow little more than sheep and heather, and the further the farmer gets from the east coast, the more likely he is to be ploughing shallow soil. But even in the west, when the land begins to rise, the dales run rich and fertile up between the fells. Most of Yorkshire is clouded hills and pastures green. The dark Satanic mills are pushed away into the corners of the county.

When Sheffield was a village, Leeds a parish and Halifax and Huddersfield hamlets, if they existed at all, the great sweep of rural Yorkshire flowered and flourished. It was powerful as well as prosperous, wise as well as wealthy; the natural home of the Augustine, Cistercian, Benedictine and Carthusian monks who prayed and proselytised in mediaeval England. For the contemplative orders who hoped to meditate their way to heaven, far from the world and its temptations, Yorkshire provided a refuge. For the zealots who wanted to plant Christ's flag in every market place, Yorkshire offered a challenge.

Looking back over north-west Yorkshire from the top of Sutton Bank it is easy to believe that the communities which moved into the vales of Wharfe, Aire and Nidd chose security as well as salvation. Behind are the north York moors, too high to be really hospitable. But below is the mirror image of the view from the Harrogate to Ripon Road. The fertile fields are exactly the right setting for merry monks and fat friars—but that is not how it was when the great Abbeys were founded. The twelve monks who left York and St Mary's Benedictine comfort to live a life of Cistercian austerity, walked west into a wilderness. Where they settled is now light and green and beautiful—not least because the Brothers of Fountains Abbey laboured to make it so. Fountains Abbey has been a ruin for four hundred years. But it is a ruin as the Acropolis and Baalbek are ruins. It is a memorial to another civilisation—its craftsmanship, its art and above all its persistence.

The best—though historically improper—way to visit Fountains is through Studley Roger and along the consciously prepossessing tree-lined avenue that leads to Studley church. It is a road in the great tradition of planned and planted English roads—designed for eighteenth-century squires to drive along without having to twitch their reins to left or right. At its end the style and the character change. In the abbey grounds, the Lords of the Manor of Studley have built themselves a little Chatsworth Park, not a place for country squires but a haven for the educated aristo-cracy of the Enlightenment. The landscaped lakes and the cultivated canals are properly precise. The Temple of Piety—ochre behind its colonnade, like a late Hapsburg hunting lodge—is clearly the result of meticulous draftsmanship. The Roman wrestlers locked in metal combat, and Hercules labouring against Antaeus, are so clearly the outcome of classical education and conscious good taste that they need protecting from rough people and rude elements by iron railings and polythene sheets. Round the corner, through the wood, Fountains Abbey is open and free to anyone who wants to walk over the close-cropped grass that grows between what is left of its once magnificent walls. Once it was the model of English mediaeval ecclesiastical architecture. Yet it has no period. In ruins it proclaims virtues that defy time and style.

Years of dogged and detailed devotion were more important than moments of sudden inspiration in the building of Fountains. After every flush of genius there had to follow years of aching muscles and torn hands. Fountains was built in praise of God and keeping going, and during the decades of addition and improvement it changed from a little shrine in the forest huddled against the hill to a city in itself spreading across the flat green valley of the Skell.

The first monks built modestly from local stone. Their successors had greater ambition. They built the nave and the choir, and beyond the

choir the Chapel of Nine Altars with its great east windows. They built
a chapterhouse and a refectory, and a long cellarium with vaulted roof
and centre pillars. They built an infirmary for the monks and another for
the lay brothers, a guest house for strangers and all the pantries and
kitchens that a community of a thousand souls could reasonably require,
complete with tall chimneys that took the smoke, if not to heaven, at
least out of the bakeries and above the dormitories. And fifty years before
the monasteries were dissolved they built the perfect perpendicular tower.

The Reformation ended four hundred years of continuous building. It
took extraordinary men to dress and lay each piece of stone and labour
to add the extra cubit to an abbey that had gradually grown for two or
three hundred years. The work could only be done if each humble task
was an individual achievement; a proof of craftsmanship and a demonstra-
tion of devotion in itself. Every monk and mason knew that the work
would never be done. There was always something else to be added for
the glory of God and in celebration of human achievement. The monks of
Fountains believed that they could work themselves to heaven. Given
another four hundred years they would have covered half Yorkshire with
their gothic arches.

Henry VIII interrupted the work that should have lasted for eternity.
The swift, formal Dissolution of the Monasteries and the three hundred
years of casual neglect which followed turned much of Fountains Abbey
into roofless walls and mounds of earth where altars used to stand. But
in ruins the Abbey has a unique magnificence—the suggestion of what
once was there as awe-inspiring as the reality of what remains. It is easy
to understand why the men who inhabited it heard the clear and constant
call of duty.

One of the duties of monastic life was to go forth and collectively
multiply. St Mary's begat Fountains. Fountains begat Kirkstall. And, as
part of a different line, Embsay begat Bolton in the valley of the Wharfe.
The Augustines at Bolton lasted a year longer than the Cistercians at
Fountains. Indeed dissolution came only just in time. Abbot Moore had
almost finished his new west tower when the King's messenger arrived.
Had the desecration been delayed another year the early English front of
the old Abbey would have been covered over and forgotten. Thanks to
Anne Boleyn, the Abbey was spared that destructive improvement.

That Bolton was never finished was a blessing. Its beginning was a
benefaction. According to Wordsworth, the "stately Priory was raised"
because a greyhound (the sort that tugs at Diana, not the kind that goes
with cloth caps and mufflers) pulled the Boy of Egremont into the Strid—

a chasm only four feet wide, where the Wharfe runs fast and ten feet deep before it wanders, slow and shallow, past the abbey. His mother founded the priory as his memorial.

Across the river on the Hill of the Standard, Francis Norton, another Wordsworth hero, fell, stabbed "from behind with treacherous wound" in defence of family, fortune and the north of England. But on a warm Whit Monday evening, there is nothing menacing about the Wharfe at Bolton and the hills that hem it in. Paddling children wobble their way across the pebbles of the river bed. On its banks a dozen cricket matches overlap.

In the Devonshire Arms, the prefabricated gift shop in the car park and the Post Office and general store in its little garden, business is brisk. The neglect of winter is forgotten and the cash registers combine in a continuous carillon. Abbeys are obviously a good investment. When Abbot Moore handed Bolton to the Crown in 1540, its annual income was £390. To a King interested in theft as well as theology, that made it a better prospect than Rievaulx. Although high on the north York moors Rievaulx at Old Bylands should have been worth more than £351 a year. In 1131 the valley of the Rye was "a place of Horror and waste solitude". By 1167, because of hard work and fast building, there were so many monks and lay brothers within its walls that "the church swarmed with them like a hive of bees". Originally there had been two Abbeys in the valley. On the right bank Savigniac monks lived on land given them by Roger de Mowbray. On the left bank, Cistercians enjoyed the benefice of Walter l'Espec. The arrangement proved unsatisfactory. Each monastery was confused by the other's bells—"which was not fitting and could not be endured". Graciously the Savigniac monks agreed to up altar and move to Stocking. But they still owned the right bank and virtually all the flat floor of the valley. For the Rye ran close against the left-hand slope and all that could be ploughed and planted lay on the Savigniac side. Gradually, by cunning and by contract, the course of the river was changed. Sometimes the bank was moved surreptitiously to the right. Sometimes the river was drained and shifted by agreement. By the end of the thirteenth century, Rievaulx—the monastery which remained—owned all the land from Penny Piece to Ashberry Hill. Its writ still only ran as far as the Rye, so the abbot remained lord of only the left bank. But the river had been pushed hard up against the western slope. All that was fertile now lay on its left. Beyond the right bank was thick forest and steep hill. It had taken the monks several lifetimes to move the river. But they had all the time which the world could provide. Their strength was the willingness to work on until the last trumpet sounded like a factory hooter to signify that man's little working day was over.

The Cistercians of Rievaulx were indomitable in their determination to make the valley worthy of this work and worship. The Savigniacs were indefatigable in their willingness to search the north of England for a home which did justice to their creed and calling. They began at Furness in Lancashire. Roger de Mowbray's gift tempted them across the Pennines and they established a house at Old Bylands on the Rye. Then there was the confusion of bells and conflict of convenience with their brothers across the stream. So they moved on and began to build again at Stocking. They ended their travels on the southern slopes of the Hambledon Hills. It took years to drain the land before the building could begin. To the monks, the moves from place to place were just another part of the service to the Lord. They built and rebuilt. At every stop, they called the infant abbey "Bylands". They had come to Yorkshire to build Bylands to the Glory of God. Forty years and three sets of foundations later, neither the name or the task had changed.

The triumph of work as well as worship was celebrated in every monastery in Yorkshire. At Gisborough the monks pulled down the Norman priory simply for the joy of replacing it in the Decorated style. At Whitby, Caedmon proved that by application a humble ploughman could become a great poet. He was helped by divine revelation and the patronage of St Hilda, but from the dream onwards he was singing the story of the Creation and Redemption fourteen hours a day. The abbey that his patron founded on the windswept site of a Roman signal station was host to the great Synod of 664. There were long days of disputation and competitive logic and conflicting theology. The Synod of Whitby had to choose between the rival merits of the Celtic and Roman rites. In the end St Peter's legion won and the English church was set in its ways for almost nine hundred years.

The abbey—ravaged by Danes and attacked by Norwegians—survived as long as the Roman Mass. It was dissolved on December 14th, 1539. Its estimated value on the day of its confiscation was £437-2-9. Within a month of its surrender to the King's Commissioner, it was leased to Richard Cholmley of Pickering. True to his Yorkshire nature, he bought the freehold at the first opportunity. Whitby was a valuable property, with an annual income second in Yorkshire only to Kirkstall, where the monks had begun the great tradition of Leeds by making a fortune out of wool. Thanks to hard graft, Kirkstall was worth £500 a year.

Deo adjuvante labor proficit is the motto of half the industrial towns in

Yorkshire. People who could actually turn the moral into money have always endeared themselves to a county that wanted piety to show a profit. So Yorkshire admired the monks and loved the old religion and when Henry closed and confiscated their monasteries, Yorkshire rose up in the Pilgrimage of Grace.

The dissolution of the monasteries was neither the first nor the most terrible act of ecclesiastical destruction to have been visited on Yorkshire. William of Normandy, "harrying the North" in revenge for earlier rebellion and determination that the rebels should not rise again, devastated all the land from the Humber to the Tyne. No house was left standing, no horse or human left alive. In the Domesday Book half of north Yorkshire is marked "wasteland".

On that wasteland Saxon churches had once stood. From it the great Norman cathedrals grew. Thomas of Bayeux laid the first Norman stones at Ripon. Much of the work of his successor, Roger, Pont L'Eveque still stands—heavy and permanent, determinedly intact in a see of ruined abbeys and dissolved monasteries—looking as if the money ran out just before it was finished according to a grand and complicated design. In fact, it was finished over and over again and became the most constantly and carefully restored church in Yorkshire, with a central tower so changed and improved that it is one style up the northern side and another down the southern. But the east front, without saint or statue, seems made for decoration that the diocese could not afford and the squat west towers create an irresistible impression that they were planned to reach fifty feet nearer to heaven. In fact it was all done according to the dreams and desires of England's "second oldest city". If more money had been wanted, devout Yorkshiremen would have provided it. They were prepared to live and die for their church, pay for its glory and fight for its continuation.

On Skipworth Moor in 1536 it was fighting and dying that Robert Aske demanded of the men who marched with him to save the monasteries. The Pilgrimage of Grace had no hope of defeating the King and his castles. The price the pilgrims paid for defence of the holy houses was lifelong exile or savage execution.

They captured Pomfret Castle. They besieged Skipton, Whitby and Scarborough, kneeling outside the castle walls in prayer for supernatural reinforcement. The Mayor and Commoners of Doncaster swore an oath of adhesion to their cause. But these were local triumphs, the little victories of an amateur army. When the Duke of Norfolk and his professional soldiers rode north, the Pilgrimage disintegrated. But the devotion of Yorkshire to the old Christianity and to the priests and monks who laboured for its great glory had been established for ever. In Yorkshire piety is still respected, determination still admired and hard work still revered. No doubt, in heaven they have similar values. When the monks of Fountains, Rievaulx, Bylands and Bolton arrived, they must have found it just like home.

FIVE

Conflict and Art

SKYLARK'S SONG

On the afternoon of Easter Sunday 1975 the rain fell on Haworth in a particularly Yorkshire way. It was neither extreme nor spectacular. But it was determined. It soaked the just and the unjust alike. It fell straight and certain on the steam engines of the Keighley and Worth Valley Railway Preservation Society and on its prospective passengers who stood, amongst the Victorian rolling stock, in small damp groups, exuding the special smell of warm wet wool.

A quarter of a mile away up past Rochester Building and the Brontë Hairdressing Salon, through the old village at the top of the hill, the holiday makers endured a different quality of rain. It did not simply come down. It blew from across the moors, horizontal and hostile, challenging the anoraks and pakamacs head on. It bent round the corners of the Victorian houses and spread across the black cobblestones of Main Street, making them shine like the toe-cap of a guardsman's boot. The queue that ended at the front door of Haworth Parsonage stood firm.

They stood—not Americans with movie cameras and checked golf trousers but ordinary Yorkshiremen in ordinary Yorkshire clothes— quiet and orderly, stretching out across the Parsonage's flag-stoned yard, through the black iron railings (which seem more designed to keep people in than sheep out) and down the rough road that the Reverend Patrick Brontë walked each day between home and church. On one side were the great grey granite tombstones, lying flat in the churchyard like stone-age table tops. On the other was the school-house, where Charlotte Brontë taught the gospel on Sundays. Between the Sunday School and the burial ground the silent column waited, wet and patient, before them the prospect of treading where Charlotte, Emily and Anne once trod—three women who, for all their wild and timeless genius, were unmistakably the product of nineteenth-century Yorkshire.

Not Yorkshire alone, for they wrote about strange vices and improbable virtues that Haworth never knew. But the background to their melodramas—both the places and the people—is always the West Riding. The moors around Wuthering Heights and Thornfield Hall are the moors that run across the Pennines. The storms that blew through Villette are the storms that blow over the hills from Lancashire. Helen

Burns, Joseph and Mrs Dean are as much a part of Yorkshire as the rain and the heather. It is because of them—the minor characters as much as the massive landscape—that the Brontës reproduce the spirit of the Three Ridings more than any other novelist or poet.

Andrew Marvell represented Kingston-upon-Hull in Parliament, but he longed to be "where the remote Bermudas ride". J. B. Priestley caricatured his native county and convinced the southern suburbs that the dragons marked on maps of the north wore clogs and cloth caps. Alderman Mrs Beddows still serves on councils all over the county, but half of Winifred Holtby's characters are as fictitious as the South Riding itself. Only the Kingsport working class are real Yorkshire. Sarah Burton's injunction to "question everything" owes more to Somerville sophistication than to Hull hard-headedness. But Emily, Charlotte and Anne wrote out their passions against the background of places and people which they understood. What they understood was moorland Yorkshire, hill country where the bleak and the beautiful are side by side offering their mutual lessons to those who live there:

> Because the road is rough and long
> Shall we despise the skylark's song?

I discovered that people wrote about Yorkshire during my twelfth year. In form x of the Sheffield City Grammar (x was a concession to parity of esteem; b would have confirmed our inferior status to a) we were given battered copies of *More Essays by Modern Masters*. By 1946 they were no longer modern. They wrote about a world divided from mine by time and class distinction. But reading them changed my life. I had no doubt that if I could neither play cricket for Yorkshire nor football for Sheffield Wednesday I wanted to be Robert Lynd or Hilaire Belloc, writing rounded essays, whole and complete in their two thousand words, pure polished and perfect.

Halfway through the dog-eared pages was *T'Match* by J. B. Priestley. It was sandwiched between *On Running After One's Hat* and *The Honest Man and the Devil*. In proper Yorkshire style I preferred the bread to the filling in the middle. *T'Match* was about the wrong sort of football and was old-fashioned about Rugby League, which it called "Northern Union". But it did contain one paragraph which I understood.

It is a country, whether it expresses itself in fields or streets, moors or mills, that puts a man on his mettle. It defies him to live there, and so it has to be a special race that lives there, stocky men with short upper lips, jutting long chins, men who roll a little in their walk and carry their heads stiffly, twelve stones of combative instinct. If you have never seen any of these men, take a look at the Yorkshire cricket team next summer. Or come to t'match.

It was the first time that I had thought of Yorkshire as a combative county, the beginning of my understanding of why we played to win and despised good losers. From that moment on, I have never doubted how Yorkshire's character was formed. It was, I suppose, my first exposure to "the cult of Northernness" which so enraged George Orwell that he wrote (I am told ironically) what still seems to me a simple description of undisputed fact.

A Yorkshireman in the South will always take care to let you know that he regards you as an inferior. If you ask him why he will explain that it is only in the North that life is "real" life, that the industrial work done in the North is the only "real" work, that the North is inhabited by "real" people, the South merely by rentiers and their parasites. The Northerner has "grit", he is grim, "dour", plucky, warm-hearted and democratic, the Southerner is snobbish, effeminate and lazy.

Exactly, and it comes out in what we write—not in what is written about us by envious outsiders, but in what is written by Yorkshire men and women who know Yorkshire and by those who are prepared to take the trouble to stay and to learn. When Mrs Gaskell arrived at Haworth to write her *Life of Charlotte Brontë* she found Yorkshiremen "interesting as a race" but "at the same time, as individuals, the remarkable degree of self-sufficiency which they possess gives them an air of independence rather apt to repel a stranger". But Mrs Gaskell learned. A few weeks after she had stepped off the train at Keighley she was writing of "strong sagacity and the dogged purpose of will which seems almost a birthright to the natives of the West Riding". By the time she returned to Knutsford she had got it about right. "The affections are strong and their foundations lie deep; but they are not—such affections seldom are—wide spreading; nor do they show themselves on the surface."

But whilst Yorkshire emotions and affections are deeply submerged, Yorkshire industry is instantly visible to every traveller. In 1830 William Cobbett saw the "iron furnaces in all the horrible splendour of their ever-lasting blaze". A hundred years after Cobbett had ridden past "the yellow waves of fire" George Orwell saw "fiery serpents of steel being hauled to and fro by redlit boys" and heard "the whizz and thump of steam hammers and the scream of hammers under the blow". Despite Cobbett's attachment to the old rural virtues that he pretended once flourished in England he was caught by the moment of golden splendour amongst the grey squalor. Despite Orwell's hatred of the pain and indignities endured by the labouring poor, in the glow of the furnace, for a second, the furnacemen were magic figures. In the hardest and worst of industrial Yorkshire, there was always something magnificent to be found by travellers willing to look for it.

J. B. Priestley was born and bred in the county. For him there is no credit in understanding Yorkshire, no excuse for error and inaccuracy. I have never forgiven him for the embarrassment I always felt at his attempts to reproduce the Yorkshire dialect. I knew that apostrophes did not appear in every Yorkshire sentence and I suspected that Mr Priestley knew it too. I heard him reading the *Postscript* on the Sunday night wireless.

Priestley's Yorkshiremen produce their strangest sounds at football matches. Yet the football supporters of *The Good Companions* went to the match for reasons I totally understood.

> To say that men paid their shillings to watch twenty-two hirelings kick a ball is merely to say that a violin is wood and catgut, that *Hamlet* is so much paper and ink. For a shilling the Bruddersford United A.F.C. offered you Conflict and Art.

That is a perfect description of Yorkshire pretension about ball games. The elevation of competitive sport into a moral exercise. The insistence that cricket is a spiritual experience and football the model of the good combative life. The county and its games cannot be separated. When southern poets dreamed of home from Flanders, their dream was

> ... of a small and firelit room
> With yellow candles burning straight
> And glowing pictures in the gloom,
> And kindly books that hold me late.

But Yorkshiremen had other memories of England, home and beauty:

> We ate our breakfast lying on our backs
> Because the shells were screeching overhead

I bet a rasher to a loaf of bread
That Hull United would beat Halifax
When Jimmy Stainthorpe played full-back instead
Of Billy Bradford. . . .

Conflict and art: art and conflict, the two things are inseparable parts of life in the combative county.

But that is not all. Yorkshire is a county of ostentatious virtue and visible piety—and John Wesley was fêted all the way from Harrogate in the west to Scarborough in the east to prove it. Anyone who did not believe in redemption by published good works and damnation as the certain result of debt and dissipation could neither reflect the substance nor the spirit of Yorkshire.

Helen Burns ("it is far better to endure patiently a smart that nobody else feels but you rather than to commit a hasty action whose evil consequences will extend to all connected with you") sprays the early pages of *Jane Eyre* with uplifting advice that might have been the texts of a thousand sermons preached in a self-righteous county during a sanctimonious age. Coughing and dying in Lowood Institution (Yorkshire abounded in such places; up the road in Greta Bridge, Mr Wackford Squeers had just founded Dotheboys Hall) Helen met the desperate end of the Victorian middle-class orphan. But she met it with the sort of overt indomitability that Orwell found so infuriating. "It is weak and silly to say that you cannot bear what it is your fate to be required to bear."

Helen Burns is the true tragic heroine of Yorkshire literature, certain of eternal life in a West Riding heaven, triumphing over a hard, cold inhospitable world, but a paragon against whose life the conduct of the soft south can be measured and found wanting. In the fictitious world she inhabited virtue is not always rewarded; but guilt is always exposed, sin is always punished, forbidden love always discovered. Ask Heathcliff and Cathy. Ask Jane and Mr Rochester. Ask Jess Oakroyd or Sarah Burton. Ask even Joe Lampton. But do not ask John Braine. I remember him explaining to me the true message and real moral of *Room at the Top* and discovering how much better was the novel I had read than the one he had written.

Joe Lampton's Warley, like Jess Oakroyd's Bruddersford and Sarah Burton's Kingsport, were places that I recognised. They were caricatures of Yorkshire, but they were Yorkshire nevertheless. I recognised the moors around Thornfield Hall ("ripe bilberries gleaming here and there like jet beads") and the weather in Villette ("rain like spray and sometimes a sharp hail like shot"). It was the essentially Yorkshire detail in *Wuthering Heights* that worried Charlotte about her sister's novel. In her preface to the second edition she describes the "faults" which would be found in it by "strangers who ... unacquainted with the locality where the scene of the story is laid, to whom the inhabitants, the customs, the natural characteristics of the outlying hills and hamlets in the West Riding of Yorkshire are things alien and unfamiliar.... To all such, " Charlotte feared, "*Wuthering Heights* must appear a rude and strange production. The wild moors of the north of England can for them have no interest, the language, the very dwellings and household customs of the scattered inhabitants of those districts, must be to such readers in great measure unintelligible, and—where intelligible—repulsive."

Charlotte underestimated the universality of Emily's appeal and the attraction that the moors and mores of northern England have in the softer south. Even George Orwell conceded that "the Southerner goes north, at any rate for the first time, with the vague inferiority-complex of a civilised man venturing amongst savages". The longer the stranger stays, the less savage Yorkshire seems. Those who live there it holds tight and close, and it convinces the most turbulent of its children that there is nothing softer than millstone grit and nothing warmer than the rain which blows across Haworth Moors. Out on those moors even Heathcliff and Catherine found eventual peace and inspired the incomparable epitaph for Yorkshire:

I lingered then, under the benign sky: watched the moths fluttering among the heath and harebells, listened to the soft wind breathing through the grass, and wondered how anyone could ever imagine unquiet slumbers for sleepers in that quiet earth.

GET STUCK IN!

FOOTBALL BEGAN FOR me on a sunlit autumn afternoon in 1944 when Sheffield Wednesday were at home to Nottingham Forest in the wartime Northern League. Nottingham was my father's town and Forest his team, so off we went to Hillsborough, me filled with hope and him full of nostalgia. Sheffield Wednesday have been my team ever since.

On their ground I experienced all the emotions that the football supporter might enjoy and must endure. Standing on their terraces, I roared my partisan passions. Sitting in the stands I properly suppressed the baser expressions of joy in victory and the cruder manifestations of defiance in defeat. Huddled behind Wednesday's goal I waited for the announcement that every schoolboy expects, but knows will never come. "Goodfellow" (or Morton or McIntosh—the fantasy survived a whole generation of goalkeepers) "has been taken ill. Will Roy Hattersley come to the players' entrance at once and bring his boots and jersey with him?" High up on Spion Kop, I learned and sang the Wednesday song:

> Roll along Sheffield Wednesday, roll along,
> Put the ball in the net where it belongs,
> When Jackie Robinson gets the ball,
> Then it's sure to be a goal,
> Roll along Sheffield Wednesday, roll along.

The lyric lacked both the literary invention and the tribal significance that scholars have discovered in the football songs of the 1970s. It did not even possess the graceful parody of Sheffield United's "Wonderful, wonderful Jimmy Hagan. . . ." But it was my song, pure blue and white. I sang away the Saturday afternoons through mouthfuls of Nuttalls' Mintoes and listened to stories of great golden days between the wars.

The late forties were the boom years of English football. England was still unbeaten at home by any foreign team. "Full Internationals" were the footballers who had competed in the Home Championship, not the players who had frolicked through ninety friendly minutes with Brazil or Argentina. The World Cup was beneath us and we were on top of the world. The European Club competition was yet to begin and the fans (their enthusuasm for real competitive football built up by years of war-time abstinence) flocked to experience the delights of Cup and League. At Hillsborough we queued from six until noon to buy a ticket for the semi-final. But when we actually witnessed the great event, it was never a Yorkshire club which won and took the glory road to Wembley. The triumphs belonged to Lancashire and London, the Midlands and the north-east.

It had not always been like that. In the twenties and thirties, when Arsenal was making history by giving its ageing players monkey glands, Yorkshire was quietly dominating Cup and League. Huddersfield won the Championship three seasons running and came a close second for the next two years. Sheffield Wednesday won the League (once by a margin of ten clear points) in successive seasons and then came third four times in a row. Sheffield United brought the Cup home to Bramall Lane in 1925, the middle of a decade of absolute Yorkshire domination, when the names which schoolboys conjured with were Stevenson, Capstick, Gillespie, Needham, Blenkinsop, Leach, Marsden and Seed.

In a game which thrives on innovation, the supremacy of Sheffield and Huddersfield could not last. The final fling (putting aside the dying fall of Wembley defeats in 1936 and 1938) was Sheffield Wednesday's Cup in Silver Jubilee year. I was wheeled down to Middlewood Road to see the victorious team come home: eleven heroes on top of an open bus, not wearing the double-breasted blazers and sharp suits of post-war idols, but dressed in the thick shirts and heavy square-toed boots which they wore on every winter Saturday afternoon.

At least, that is how I imagine it. I was two at the time. Strapped in my push-chair, I enjoyed a less than perfect view of the triumphant homecoming. But of one thing I am certain. The victorious captain holding the Cup aloft for all but the smallest and most restricted spectator to see, was Ron Starling. I know because we talked about it in his paper shop during the dismal football days of the 1950s. We bought our papers there to ensure that, during an adolescence in which I was denied no advantage, I should handle a *Manchester Guardian* handed to me by a man who had held the FA Cup.

It was nearly forty years before a Yorkshire club brought home the Cup again. Between the end of the war and Leeds United's great epoch, Yorkshire supporters had to be content with teams which won no honours, the occasional international who lost his place as soon as he won his cap, the potential star who shot into a new firmament the moment that news of his sparkle and shine penetrated the light years between Yorkshire and football's higher galaxies, and the faded glory of great names who added a touch of retrospective distinction to teams in the Third and Second Divisions.

For Doncaster Rovers to have the ageing Peter Docherty on their playing staff was probably the greatest achievement in the club's history. Horatio Carter's silver hair and long shorts never really suited the greyhound-track-encircled pitch at Boothferry Road. But no one like him has played for Hull City before or since. Only in the far north-east, at Ayresome Park, were regular contemporary internationals on view in Yorkshire. Hardwick—immaculate in appearance as well as style—was permanent left back for Middlesbrough and England. Wilf Mannion, his club colleague, was only left out of the national team when injury or the inability of the selectors to recognise true genius denied him his rightful place. But for ten years after Hardwick and Mannion had gone, Yorkshire internationals either faded and were dropped, or prospered and passed on to more successful clubs.

Barnsley became a human clearing house for footballers on their way from exotic and unlikely places to football fame and fortune. The Robledo brothers called in between Chile and Newcastle in Cup year. The Blanchflowers of Belfast passed through en route to London and Manchester. Some Yorkshire clubs discovered local prodigies and sold their talents to stay solvent. Len Shackleton won his first England cap at Bradford and moved to Sunderland to join Jackie Robinson, late of Sheffield Wednesday. Others scouted the country for incipient heroes, found and developed them and cashed in their investment. So Alex Forbes blossomed for Sheffield United, but bore fruit for Arsenal. No sooner had Yorkshire schoolboys begun to identify with their heroes, copy their mannerisms and aspire to their achievements than the great men moved on and took their glory with them.

The Yorkshire schoolboys had no real cause for complaint. The football supporter's loyalty has to be to a name and a ground not to a team. The club players on whose success his Saturday evening happiness depends are the best that transfer fees and bonuses can buy. They are mercenaries, fighting for money and love of battle, with no permanent allegiance to any standard, who rally round today's flag because that is what they are paid to do. Although Wednesday was my local team, I never thought of it as part of my local heritage. There was nothing especially Yorkshire about the football they played—no special Yorkshire style, tradition, grace or virtue that distinguished it from football played across the Pennines or south of the Humber. It took twenty years of unswerving support to discover that a real Yorkshire pulse throbbed at least through the two Sheffield teams. The heartbeat could—and still can—be recorded, in the Directors' box.

Football Directors are nobody's friends except when there are Cup Final tickets to give away, but they represent continuity whether the club fails or flourishes in a way that transient players and insecure managers cannot. They spring from the local soil, take root and often became impossible to dislodge even when the sap no longer rises and the leaves are brown and withered. They are the team's spirit, its tradition, its continuity.

At Bramall Lane and Hillsborough, continuity is so well preserved that the door marked "Directors Only" is the entrance to a football time-machine which rolls the world back fifty years. Of course, physically, both grounds have seen mighty changes. At Hillsborough the great World Cup stand is a memorial to the years when Sheffield Wednesday sank from the First to the Third Division. At Bramall Lane, the Yorkshire Cricket Club have been evicted and United have built across where the wicket used to be, where the bombs fell in 1940 and where the Hallamshire Battalion mustered in 1914. And on the improved and expanded grounds a new generation of players call their shirts "strip", the pitch "the park" and talk apparently knowledgeably about "purposive running" and "peripheral vision". All that is new. But when the Directors meet on match days the spirit has not changed since the twenties.

It is a place where men understand their relative station in life and women accept that they are different. Directors themselves and guests of special distinction stir tea and drink whisky in protected seclusion. Other visitors eat and drink identical victuals but consume them separately because, in a hierarchical world, that is the natural order of things. Ladies—whatever their rank, class, achievement or eminence—are automatically excluded from the first order of football society, with only one exception. A lady Lord Mayor becomes, as far as both Wednesday and United are concerned, a man whenever she wears her chain of office. Other ladies are treated with complicated courtesy and meticulous respect. They are given particularly thick rugs to protect them from the cold and extraordinarily thin sandwiches to spare them the pork pie and cold sausages. The idea that the fur-coated ladies of Sheffield football are inferior to anyone in the world has never passed through their hatted heads. But they would no more expect to drink with their husbands at half-time than they would aspire to sit with them during the match.

For a man who spent his boyhood on Spion Kop, an invitation to sit in the Wednesday Directors' Box was like a Royal Command. I already knew the "Royal Family". Eric Taylor—"football's longest serving manager"—was our neighbour. We admired his durability and his canniness. For years he painted his house in blue and white stripes. In bad years after the war (and there were many), dissident fans would be told about the loyalty of his decorations and would instantly accept that a man of such obvious devotion was indispensable to the club. It was Mrs Taylor who suggested that a young Scot—recently arrived from Edinburgh and making ends meet as Sheffield Wednesday's doctor— might find the cure for my bronchitis that had already eluded a succession of GPs. Twenty years later he was introducing the Queen to Cup Finalists at Wembley: Sir Andrew Stephen, Chairman of the Football Association.

But nodding to neighbours and coughing for doctors was one thing. Meeting them in their glory as the men behind the team, behind almost every other team in the Second Division, was quite another. We did not come straight from the wet and weather-beaten terraces. On the day I tried to put my umbrella up behind Manchester United's goal my father and I agreed that he was too old and I was too decadent for the concrete steps. Indeed, the Mancunians, whose view I obscured, made much the same point, though in different language. So we bought tickets for the extremity of the old stand and squinted from our seats over the corner flag. But we were still unprepared for the padded seats and the heated footrests of the first four rows at the centre line.

We gave up Nuttalls' Mintoes. We learned to stroll nonchalantly into the ground at five to three rather than rush at the turnstile at quarter past two. We sat prim and proper and boasted to each other that we had watched Wednesday from every part of the ground. But I never felt confident in the exalted company until the late sixties. Then, with Yorkshire two hundred miles and five years behind me, I followed the Club and its Directors on their visit to London grounds and relaxed in all the friendly familiarity of exiles in an alien land.

In January 1974 I arrived at Stamford Bridge, a hanger-on with the Sheffield Wednesday visitors. I was late for my rendezvous. A minute before the kick-off I stood blinking at the back of the Directors' Box, adjusting my eyes to the light and deciding where to sit. On my left was carefully cut hair, brushing the back of corduroy suits and touching the velvet collars of cavalry coats. On the right were heads cropped as close as boil-scars would allow. I recognised the men with graces but with few airs, men of property, who had no intention of flaunting or wasting what they had earned. I had no doubt which side I was on.

At the end of the match we all went to drink together—not just the victorious and vanquished directors linked in a moment of mock modesty and bogus sportsmanship, but wives and daughters, joining men with serious business to discuss and serious results from other grounds to ponder. Chelsea beat Wednesday 3–2. But as we say in Yorkshire (after we have lost), "Some things are more important than winning."

BEFORE THE FALL

BETWEEN THE TWO Great Wars, there was only one cricket team in England. During twenty years of peace, Yorkshire won the Championship twelve times and for three summers arrived at September and the Scarborough Cricket Festival unbeaten by either rival county or visiting country team. Yorkshire's inter-war supremacy was the great bridging passage in English cricket which linked the infant glory of the Edwardian game with the era of falling gates and the need for entertainment which came in with the affluent fifties. During the two inter-war decades there was more talent in the county than the club could accommodate—some of it the literal product of the years before the lights went out. But the unremitting victories of the twenties and thirties were as much a triumph for temperament as for talent—and the temperament of those victorious teams had little in common with the studiously cultivated carefree grace of cricket's "golden age".

The golden age of English cricket is rarely described in the precise statistics of matches won, runs scored and wickets taken. Historians of the period are usually more literate than numerate. Contemporary observers wrote of it in prose which was invariably lyrical. Retrospective accounts are universally elegiac. During the sunlit summers of the century's first decade, declarations were always sporting. Flannels were unfailingly cream and carefully creased. Silk shirts—though modestly buttoned—always rippled in the wind as batsmen bent to take guard. Elegance was an end in itself. Style and sportsmanship were the major virtues. Batsmen cut and cover-drove even when the ball was new and the wicket green. It was the age of the "gentleman"; Warner, Fry, Jessop and MacLaren—the last being the most legendary and least successful of all England's captains.

In 1901, MacLaren—the spirit of the age—actually took a team to Australia which did not include a single Yorkshireman. Australia won four of the five Test Matches and the MCC decided that, in future, the selection of touring teams could not be left to the patrician foibles of the Captain. As a result Wilfred Rhodes and George Hirst became permanent adornments of the England side, but although a product of the golden age, they were never typical of it. All that was Yorkshire in them prevented that. Their superiority was not effortless and they strained neither nerve nor sinew to pretend that it was. They were as interested in winning as in playing the game. Their cautious agreement to "get 'em in singles" has become part of cricket's folk-lore. But the attitude it revealed is hardly consistent with the arcadian bliss of balmy Edwardian afternoons.

Wilfred Rhodes batted with F. S. Jackson and bowled against Victor Trumper, but he possessed durable talents which survived the First World War and bloomed and blossomed a second time. Throughout the twenties Rhodes opened Yorkshire's batting and established the great tradition of left-arm spin bowling—the meticulously set field; the precisely flighted ball of impeccable length, the tactical plan of each over merging into the strategy of the long bowling spell. In the thirties that tradition—in Yorkshire and for England—passed to Hedley Verity. Both Rhodes and Verity were brilliant but neither was flashy. Both were geniuses not journeymen, but they exploited their genius with a journeyman's power of application. And they had batsmen of concentrated brilliance to support them. Between the wars, Yorkshire always provided England with at least one opening batsman. Rhodes himself, Herbert Sutcliffe, Leonard Hutton are on every knowledgeable schoolboy's shortlist for the greatest opening batsmen of all time. Holmes and Mitchell, if not in the same class, scored a lot of runs and took a lot of shine off new balls in the process.

In 1939, Yorkshire at least seemed invincible. The year before, the young Len Hutton had batted against Australia for thirteen hours and twenty minutes and scored 364 runs. Maurice Leyland had made a century in the same Test Match. Bill Bowes had opened the bowling and entered into a passionate argument with Hedley Verity about their relative distinction as batsmen and the consequent right to appear on the score-card at number ten rather than eleven. Arthur Wood, selected at the last minute to keep wicket in place of the injured Leslie Ames of Kent, hailed a taxi in Leeds City Square and insisted that it drove him straight to the Oval. Yorkshire was rich in character as well as ability, experience as well as hope. Young men anxious to join the ground staff had to be very good indeed. At the Bradford nets a sad seventeen-year-old called Jim Laker was advised to try his luck with a less exacting county.

In 1945 it seemed that Yorkshire had survived, despite the ravages of time and war. Hedley Verity and Roy Kilner were dead. Maurice Leyland had turned from sturdy to rotund. It was fourteen years since Bill Bowes had first bowled Bradman and fast bowlers neither travel nor keep. Len

Hutton had not simply lost six of his best batting years. He had returned
from an orthopaedic hospital with his left arm four inches shorter than it
had been before the war. For a batsman of impeccable technique such
damage to the arm which guides and leads ought to have been the end of a
career. But careers do not end so easily in Yorkshire. Len Hutton
bought a boy's bat and went to the Headingley nets to start all over
again.

In 1946—the year that First Class Cricket re-appeared in post-war
England—Yorkshire won the County Championship. Booth, who had
understudied Verity for all of his adult life, stepped into the County team
at the age of forty and took a hundred wickets in his first season. Halliday,
Yardley, Watson and Gibbs, who would have become regular players in
the early forties stepped into their rightful places. Yorkshire remained
unbeaten until the end of August. Brian Sellers was still Captain. God
was in a Yorkshire heaven. All was right and proper in the cricketing
world.

That Yorkshire was able to recover so quickly was partly the result of
its size, partly the result of the way in which it organised its cricket.
Yorkshire was the largest and most populous of all English counties. So
long as county sides were mainly and generally composed of players born
within their boundaries, Yorkshire had a numerical advantage. Even when
Lancashire recruited an Australian fast bowler and Middlesex relied on a
Scottish batsman the population balance remained on Yorkshire's side.
It was not until every other county began regularly to recruit in Karachi
and Kingston, Pretoria and Perth, that Yorkshire became outnumbered.
In the days when the overseas player was an exception, Yorkshire was the
biggest county in the Championship. When, for other counties, overseas
players became the rule, the Yorkshire County Cricket Club had,
suddenly, the smallest area of choice in the cricketing world.

But in 1946 Yorkshire was still the big battalion. And it was not only
big. Typically, it was well organised. Yorkshire cricket had begun at
Sheffield in 1863 when the city's "match committee" had expanded its
influence and authority to the whole county. Thirty years later the Club
was reformed and officially founded and set up home in Leeds where, for
half a century, it occupied premises suitable for a Victorian solicitor in
Old Bank Chambers, Park Row. But support for the Club was not
confined to the county's two major cities and enthusiastic supporters not
only paid their membership fees—they wanted Yorkshire value for
Yorkshire money. So the County side travelled even when it played at
home. Leeds and Sheffield had four matches, Bradford three, Hull two,

Harrogate one and Scarborough had the cricket festival. To sustain such a peripatetic programme it was necessary to cultivate six good wickets. On and around them, on the majority of Saturdays when there was no first-class match, were born and bred the local sides which flowed like tributaries into the mainstream of the Championship side.

In the south of England, the counties are supplied and sustained by "club cricket", a form of cricket which, for all its quality, is clearly related to good fellowship and conviviality. In the north the parallel—though hardly equivalent—institution is "league cricket", a system obviously more concerned with tables that demonstrate success and failure than with the affectionate virtues. League cricket existed outside Yorkshire. In Nottingham, colliers dreamed of escaping from the pits through the Bassetlaw League. The Lancashire League thrived on an unashamed commitment to commercial entertainment that involved the recruitment of high-priced West Indians to hit sixes and amuse the crowds. But the Yorkshire Council and the Yorkshire League were different. There the players always played to win and sometimes played for money, but they did something more. They saw themselves as the yeomanry ready to support the regular army that battled for Yorkshire in the County Championship. Each League side had close formal ties with the County HQ. Many had a county "colt" farmed out to their clubs to keep him in practice during the weeks when the Second XI had no game. The system sustained Yorkshire right into the late fifties. Then cricket began to change and Yorkshire chose not to change with it.

Faced with the necessity to raise extra cash (for the game became expensive when players demanded a living wage) and the need to compete for spectators against all the attractions of the television-owning democracy, the ancients of the MCC contrived the major irony in the history of cricket. After a hundred years of innate conservatism, they decided—almost overnight—to innovate quality out of the game. Final salvation would come, they adjudged, by making cricket a spectator sport, played not with the intention of winning but in the hope of providing entertainment. The spectator was a privileged observer no longer. His pleasure was the object of the game. And since his pleasure was related to the speed at which runs were scored and the frequency with which wickets were taken, the rules of the game had to be adjusted to encourage the sort of game which appealed to the paying public. That was not the game Yorkshire knew and they proved entirely incapable of adjusting themselves to the new rules which related success to popularity.

The innovation took two forms. The most pernicious was the decision that first-class cricketers should play village cricket on as many summer afternoons as industry could be persuaded to subsidise the matches. With innings limited to forty to sixty overs the game was transformed. For bowlers "keeping the runs down" became more important than taking wickets. Batsmen were forced to play shots coyly described by radio commentators as "not in the book".

When, during the early sixties, the scramble for runs was confined to the special competitions of Sundays and occasional weekdays, Yorkshire spirit and stamina survived adjustment from hit-and-run to proper cricket. But the obsession to fill seats and swell takings infected even the County Championship. "Bonus points" were invented to compensate the teams which took wickets early in the game and scored extra runs before the eightieth over of the first innings. The system—intended to keep the runs flowing and the wickets tumbling at about five o'clock on a Saturday afternoon—obliged middle-order batsmen to go for the runs and made strategic bowling of the Rhodes and Verity quality quite impossible.

It was not the first change that Yorkshire cricket had proved unable to accommodate. In the thirties the professional cricketer—the "player"— had for all his abundant talent "known his place". Herbert Sutcliffe had sprinkled eau-de-cologne on his flannels and aspired to the Captaincy, but he had never thought of challenging the Committee. The players of post-war cricket were made of a different material. Johnny Wardle (in the tradition if not of the style of Rhodes and Verity), publicly criticised by the club, retaliated in print. He was never allowed to play for Yorkshire again. Raymond Illingworth, anxious for a three-year contract and a measure of security, was told that a year with Yorkshire ought to be worth an eternity with any other county. He did not agree. He got his contract with Leicestershire and became Captain of England.

Other Yorkshiremen were even penalised and punished for articulating the traditional Yorkshire virtues. When Brian Close was excommunicated for sins—not against the Holy Ghost but against Brian Sellers (which was a much more serious crime in the County Club), amongst the liturgy of faults was his opposition to the "new cricket" that the MCC had invented. Close was not a stolid opening batsman or a stock bowler who needed three days of mediocre unimaginative effort. He was one of the most exciting cricketers of his time. His shortcoming was the willingness to dare too much rather than avoid the cricketer's gamble. He was also an archetypal Yorkshireman, concerned with competition that is genuine rather than contrived, the pursuit of the meritorious rather than the meretricious, the preservation of quality and the contempt of pretence. The Yorkshire County Cricket Club has attempted to accept cricket's new standards. But to its credit, as Close would no doubt agree, it has failed.

GLAD TIDINGS TO ZION

IT IS ADVENT in Huddersfield and it is Friday. British Rail's illuminated red and white trade-mark shines out from under the corinthian columns of the palladian railway station. But the night is so black that the peristyle which the trade-mark defiles, the magnificent colonnade which completes the classical façade, and the embossed armorial bearings of the Huddersfield and Manchester Railway and Canal Company, are invisible from the front door of the George Hotel across the corner of the square. Down Northgate, past the Orchid Club and the Rawlins School of Dancing, two hundred sopranos and tenors, basses and altos are sitting in what used to be a Primitive Methodist School. It is now the Long Street YMCA and the old school hall has a floor smooth enough for badminton, and walls pitted and mottled by a thousand basket balls. The hall is the traditional practice room of the Huddersfield Choral Society. Friday is traditional practice night and December is the traditionally busy month. Framed by a scar in the plaster where once a roll of honour or table of merit hung, Douglas Robinson OBE, shirt-sleeved behind his music stand, attempts to improve the apparently perfect.

Douglas Robinson is much more concerned about the words than the music. He knows that the Choral Society can sing and that most of its members have sung together with spectacular success for the last ten years. He finds fault or suggests improvement in the quiet certainty that "we can put it right immediately we are conscious of it", relying on both the natural talent and acquired professionalism of the Members who pay three pounds a year for the privilege of singing with the Society. Douglas Robinson was Choir Master at Covent Garden for most of the thirty years after he left Leeds, and he guides the Society through its rehearsal with accomplished control. But he articulates the evangelical zeal that comes naturally to a Society whose roots are buried deep in the Nonconformist Movement. "Exciting" is his greatest compliment. "Excitement" is the promise he holds out as the reward for getting it exactly right. Halfway through "And the Glory of the Lord . . .", he stops the singing with a short, single hand-clap that cuts across two hundred minds in deep concentration and four hundred lungs in full blast. "If it sounds as if you've sung it before and there is no message in it, we'd better not do it."

Most of them have sung it before. The Huddersfield Choral Society has performed Handel's *Messiah* every year since 1836. Now it does it twice a year, first for the *Subscribers*, who pay eight pounds for a good seat at each of the Society's three winter concerts, second for the paying public. The *Subscribers* fill the Town Hall, and a hundred and twenty music lovers are waiting to subscribe. The paying public queue at a ticket office that opens at seven thirty in the morning. The tickets are sold out by eight forty-five, the first to a customer who arrived at two o'clock the previous afternoon to ensure that he got the seat he wanted.

But tonight, only a few minutes of the Society's time is taken up with the *Messiah*. Handel's great Christmas oratorio is virtually ready for its audience. This Friday is principally a rehearsal for an innovation which brings together the two great strands of West Riding music. The Huddersfield Choral Society is joining the Black Dyke Mills Band for its annual Christmas Carol Concert. Roy Newsome, the band's conductor will take over the rehearsal before the evening is over. He and his wife have tiptoed into the hall. They sit unassumingly on the hard wooden bench that runs around the peeling plaster walls. They sing away with the same passionate enthusiasm as the Members of the Society. Between *Hail Smiling Morn* and *The Twelve Days of Christmas*, Douglas Robinson notices Roy Newsome and reproves his modesty. "You should have manifested yourself."

Black Dyke Mills is not the oldest brass band in Britain, but it is probably the most famous and certainly the best. Indeed, it is so good that in 1972 it was denied entry to the National Brass Band Championship to give other competitors a chance. The first British brass band was formed by a Monmouthshire ironworks in 1832. A year later, the York Waits added a brass band to its repertoire of formal entertainment available for official functions and civic occasions. That was the beginning of the "brass band movement" in Yorkshire. It is called a "movement" because it unites band after band in joyous competition and collaboration. It is a "movement" because of its imperishable connections with the other contemporary crusades: Methodism, Socialism and Temperance. In Yorkshire two bands survive from the great pioneering age—Besses o' th' Barn and the all-time champions from John Foster & Sons, Black Dyke Mills, Queensbury, Bradford. Both bands existed before Wellington won at Waterloo, but they turned to brass in the middle years of the nineteenth century. Besses o' th' Barn abandoned strings and reeds in 1853, the first year of the Belle Vue National Brass Band Championship. Black Dyke Mills joined the movement in 1855 and missed the first two competitive years. They have made up for it since, both in the National Championship, and the National Festival, which despite its more tranquil title is no less combative than the Championship.

Over the years, Black Dyke Mills bandsmen have become the amateur veterans of a hundred victorious campaigns and have performed a thousand perfect test pieces. They were amongst the eleven bands that mustered for the first Festival in 1900 and played in mass unison under the baton of Sir Arthur Sullivan. They helped raise the Crystal Palace roof with the première performance of his march *The Absent Minded Beggar*, and agreed that the proceeds from the event should be devoted to the dependants of the fifty thousand horse and foot going to Table Bay.

For the next thirty-six years the Festival remained at Crystal Palace where, at the zenith of the movement's pre-war glory, two hundred bands (not a drum between them, but every one composed of twenty-four or twenty-five bandsmen playing the stipulated range of instruments) blew their competitive blasts. After the fire melted the glass and bent the girders, the Festival moved to Alexandra Palace. The BBC drove the Festival to the Albert Hall. During the 1930s it had been vainly hoped that radio would prove the brass band's friend and take the movement into homes that had never heard of treble-tonguing. Television was an unmistakable enemy. Its cowboy films distracted little boys from practising their trombones and it expelled the Festival from Alexandra Palace.

Between the wars, all the mills in the West Riding, all the collieries in south Yorkshire and most of the factories of Sheffield, Leeds and Middlesbrough had their own brass bands. Only a few played in the hard, heady world of the National Championship and the National Festival. Their members preserved the essential amateur status by signing on as weavers, shot firers and furnacemen. But they were amateurs as Oxford and Cambridge boat-race crews were amateurs. When the day of the big race approaches they are required to row not read. In the weeks before the trial, few bandsmen who had survived to that exalted round did very much besides blow.

But the rest did a regular job for the full fifty weeks of the working year, practised in the evenings and performed when and where they could find an audience. They played at football matches, standing in a cold semi-circle across the half-way line and they played in wrought-iron municipal bandstands on warm summer afternoons. They marched with the Whit Monday processions of Sunday School Queens and Captains and they entertained at civic ceremonies before the soup and after the speeches. Playing was a pleasure, but a pleasure that had to be taken seriously. A false note was a tragedy. A cornet which did not shine was a disgrace. They saw themselves in a line which began with Joshua at Jericho and would not end until Gabriel stood with feet apart, moistened his lips and blew the perfect last trump. They were determined to keep the standard high. So they put on their austere dinner jackets or their colourful not-quite-military uniforms and polished, practised and played, practised, polished and played.

The Huddersfield Choral Society have been practising since 1836. In that year on July 15th sixteen men met at The Plough in Westgate to draw up rules for an adventure that was not to be taken lightly. Members arriving more than fifteen minutes late at the monthly meeting were to be fined threepence. Absence cost sixpence. Every member was allowed "to give his opinion after the performance of any piece of music, provided he do so in a respectable, friendly and becoming manner". But, "no one shall be allowed to stop, interrupt or make a disturbance . . . on pain of forfeiting the sum of two shillings and sixpence for every such offence, or be excluded".

Had the Society employed a chorus master back in 1836, no doubt he would have been excused the penalty for interruption. Douglas Robinson clearly accepts the obligation "to give his opinion—in a respectable, friendly and becoming manner". When the sharp hand-clap stops the singing, it is usually to encourage the society to improvement; "you know the tricks, all you have to do is to employ them". The tricks he wants them to employ most of all are the tricks which help them to articulate every syllable. He points to the corners of his mouth. "By the time we're finished I want you to be dead tired round about here." The music of *Silent Night* is perfect, but "remember 'silent' not 'silunt' ". *The Twelve Days of Christmas* "has to sound like joy piled on joy—and please don't spit on Christmas".

The Society work hard at accepting Douglas Robinson's advice. When they talk amongst themselves, they are talking about ways of improving the performance. For the rest of the rehearsal they are in deep concentration. The soloist in *The Holy City* has a pencil behind her ear. At the end of each verse she disturbs her complicated coiffure and uses the pencil to mark her score. For the final ten minutes (the rehearsal always ends at half past nine) there is hard concentration on previous mistakes. "I'm not so sure that *Silent Night* should be quite so silent." There is not a moment to pause even for a polite smile. "You're still too wet at the end of Christmas. You're getting drowned in the istmus." They probably groaned when he made that sort of joke at Covent Garden. In Huddersfield, they want to use the time going over the soggy ground again.

Throughout the rehearsal, Donald Hayward, non-singing treasurer to the Society, stands at the back of the hall. His father was President when the Society was making money from selling records, not living off interest from ancient royalties and an Arts Council grant. In his own words, Donald Hayward "makes cloth". He is immaculate in light-grey suit, white shirt and tie which—at first glance—appears to bear the emblems of the Yorkshire woollen industry. The machines woven in line across the tie are certainly textile machines. But on closer inspection, the flower that runs in parallel pattern proves not to be the Yorkshire rose. J. Hayward Ltd. is now part of the Tootal Group. The apparent white rose is the cotton flower and the tie is the Tootal tie. The woollen industry is changing in Huddersfield.

The connection between wool and the Choral Society goes back to the moment of its foundation. The men who came together in 1836 were artisans entitled under rule to "three gills of ale and bread and cheese" at every monthly meeting, but under solemn warning that "any member being intoxicated or using obscene language or calling any other member or members bye-names at any of the meetings, shall forfeit sixpence for each offence". For although artisans, the members were not the ordinary weavers of Huddersfield, and the founding fathers were determined that meetings should be conducted with a decorum suitable to their station in life. In 1836, the weavers had no time to sing, drink ale, eat bread and cheese or use obscene language.

The first decade of the nineteenth century had been a time of hope in Huddersfield. Demand for cloth—particularly scarlet cloth—was high and during the year in which Napoleon occupied Moscow, Enoch and James Taylor of Marsden introduced the Reverend Cartwright's invention into their factory. Thanks to the boom, the hand-loom weavers readily accepted the new machinery. Prosperity lasted three years. With Napoleon safe on St Helena, the first great industrial depression began. The men who made cloth in Huddersfield (certain that it was the power looms which had pauperised them) followed King Ludd as he hammered his destructive way across the West Riding. They called their massive blacksmith's hammer "Enoch" and chanted as they smashed "Enoch 'as made 'em and Enoch 'll break 'em." "Enoch" is preserved in the Tulson Textile Museum to prove how good the good old days really were.

Of course, progress and prosperity were victorious and the thirty years after the Luddite riots were the hardest in Huddersfield's history. If a weaver's family wanted to eat, every member old enough to walk worked in the mill. Often the working day lasted from seven in the morning until eleven o'clock at night. Sometimes children too tired to walk home would sleep underneath the looms. Fathers, leaving home before first light, would carry sleeping infants on their shoulders and, once inside the mill, wake them to begin the endless tasks of washing raw wool and minding simple machinery. By the time the Huddersfield Choral Society was founded, Richard Oastler's Factory Act had limited the working day of children. But servants were left "free" to strike their own individual bargains with their masters. The alternative to the sixteen-hour day was first Speenhamland and then the workhouse.

In the middle years of the nineteenth century, a Huddersfield weaver earned on average seven shillings a week. The Choral Society charged a quarterly subscription of half-a-crown. In consequence there were few real weavers in membership. In a rough and radical—and sometimes revolutionary—town, the Society became an enclave of respectability. Music might well soothe the savage breast, but, in Victorian Huddersfield, the Choral Society was not prepared to put the theory to the test. In 1842, a new regulation appeared in the rules of the Society.

> No person shall be a member of the Society who frequents the Hall of Science or any Socialist Meeting, nor shall the Librarian be allowed to lend copies of music (knowingly) belonging to the Society to any Socialist, on pain of expulsion.

Socialists, scientists and members of secular societies are no longer excluded. The men and women who join the Society today are of no single discernible type, class or persuasion. There are vestiges of old tradition—fathers sometimes recruit sons, teachers occasionally enrol pupils. But most of the members join simply to sing and because they are good at it. They are attracted by the Society's reputation—the years when it made big thick records, toured the world, sang the music of Vaughan Williams, Coleridge Taylor, Walford Davies and Hubert Parry with the composer conducting. The polished performers of the rehearsal are almost as varied in their opinions as they are in their appearance. There is a tenor with long hair falling on his shoulders and a thick steel-studded leather belt. There is an alto with a matching coat and dress and complicated hair that seems to have been sculptured from yellow meringue. There is an old lady whose black coat reaches her ankles and whose black cloche hat was fashionable in the twenties when she was in her teens. There are dozens of young women in trousers and middle-aged men in tweed jackets or worsted suits. They are all united simply by the pleasure of singing.

Of course, during its adolescence, the Society added another joy to the personal jubilation of singing for itself. It began to perform to an audience, to experience the delight of delighting others and to feel the special virtue of being judged the best in Yorkshire and therefore in the world. In a county that relishes competition and respects success, achieving membership of the Huddersfield Choral Society is an achievement comparable with playing for England or becoming a Fellow of the Royal Society. The man from Radio Sheffield, attending the rehearsal to prepare for the broadcast of the Carol Concert, recognised members whom he had met at practice with the smaller local societies who gladly contribute their best singers to the best choir in England. They are not only proud to do it. The sacrifice comes naturally to them. As Graham Fearnley, tenor and honorary secretary puts it, joining the Choral Society "is the logical thing to do in Huddersfield".

SIX

Where There's Muck

———————————

HARD AND PROUD

In my youth, I had only one unique attribute—the belief that there was something tender and romantic about Barnsley. For eighteen years, a process of subtle and insidious indoctrination conspired to convince me that the town possessed qualities that my contemporaries were too blind to see or too insensitive to understand. It began in 1935 when my father, after three years of unemployment, became a clerk at the Barnsley Labour Exchange, dispensing the dole on behalf of the Public Assistance Committee. On the day that he discovered that he was about to issue unemployment pay rather then receive it, he took his two young brothers to the pictures as a celebration. For sixpence they got Richard Tauber in *Lilac Time*. For the rest of my father's life whenever he heard the Marche Militaire he would describe the young Schubert wearing pince-nez (as he did himself) and leading a troop of children through the Vienna Woods to the tune of the "P.A.C. March". Then he would tell me the story of the bicycle.

For six months he made the journey between Barnsley and Sheffield on a bicycle with an oval front wheel. Every morning and every night, he travelled twelve miles forward and about the same distance up and down. There was no money for a better bike or even for a new front wheel. In any case working families living in south Yorkshire in the early thirties expected life to be a bumpy ride.

I first cycled to Barnsley on January 1st, 1947, on a gleaming Raleigh complete with dynamo and "Sturmey-Archer" three-speed gear. The cycle was the product of Uncle Syd's generosity and demob grant. The purpose of our visit was to watch history being made in Barnsley and the pit villages by which it is surrounded. From Wombwell to Wentworth Woodhouse (where the first Earl of Stafford acquired the characteristics which made him the most resourceful and resolute, ambitious and arrogant man in Stuart England) a new flag was being hoisted over all the collieries. And on the coal-mine gates a new notice was being nailed. "This colliery is now managed by the National Coal Board on behalf of the people." Bliss was it in that dawn to be alive, and to live near Barnsley. . . .

I saw *The Knight of the Burning Pestle* in Barnsley when the Young Vic was there on tour and I believed that the visit confirmed the town's special place in West Riding society. It was Barnsley supporters on Hillsborough's terrace who gave me my first glimpse of aboriginal Yorkshire. In Sheffield, at the southern tip of the county, Nottingham mores and Derbyshire patois clouded the clear stream of Yorkshire culture. But Barnsley was heartland, not border country. Uncontaminated by the world outside, they talked about their players "laking" football not playing it. They completed my education and confirmed my heritage.

And when I went to Bramall Lane and saw Collinridge on Sheffield United's left wing—professional footballer and nephew to Barnsley's Labour MP—I knew that in that place all the virtues and all the graces coincided. Even at nineteen (more suave and sophisticated than I have ever been before or since) I was the only delegate at a student conference not to laugh when the visiting Nigerian began: "Gentlemen, I come to you straight from a great international festival of culture and art, held this year in Barnsley."

Of course, as well as fantasising about Barnsley, I knew what the town was really about. Sheffield had few pits of its own, but in its northern suburbs and villages lived men who worked at the face in the South Yorkshire coalfields. They were not like the cultivated colliers of Wales who sing and write poetry. Nor were they the brutal and passionate miners who, according to D. H. Lawrence, hack their way under Eastwood. They were simply men who kept their hair cut short so that the coal dust could be easily washed out, men with blue scars on their faces, where the coal dust had stayed in. During the dark days of the forties and early fifties they came home from the pits still black, carrying their "snap tins" and their helmets. They hated the pits, but they genuinely believed that no other job was real work for a man.

The collier's relationship with coal was a gigantic paradox, a massive contradiction. He swore that his son would do something better and cleaner, and willingly paid the rates which sustained the county grammar schools of the coalfields—Wath, Penistone, Ecclesfield, Mexborough. He struggled to escape, if necessary by signing on for three years in the Guards (South Yorkshire is still a major recruiting area for the Coldstreams) with the hope that his service with the colours would get him a place in the local police force and enable his remaining years to be spent above ground. But he was proud to be a miner and in or out of the pits contemptuous of men who had never cut coal. The piles of "concessionary coal" which were dumped, as part of his wages, outside his front door marked him out from his neighbours. Every passer-by knew that a miner lived at that house, not a man who did a soft job in a factory, or spent his days in an office—which was hardly a job at all.

The miners—in the days before the pit-head baths and the new winding gear boxed in the cages and the cables—were the last visible signs of the tough old Yorkshire. Their cottages, running in squat grey rows along the contours of the scrub-covered hills, and the back-to-back houses in the factory towns still showed how Yorkshire families lived in the glory of Queen Victoria's England. The slag-heaps (in the forties neither flattened nor over-grown) were a visible reminder that the environment is a twentieth-century invention. The miners and industrial labourers of Yorkshire came from the enclosed common land and the entailed farms to make nineteenth-century England rich and prosperous. They lived and worked in a way which made them and their children hard—and a hundred years later the calluses still show. The way they lived and worked in Yorkshire when Britain was just becoming the damp, dirty, dangerous workshop of the world reveals as much about the county's character as anything the Brontë sisters wrote.

When Patrick Brontë was rector of Haworth, life expectancy in his parish was twenty-eight years and nine months. Four out of every ten children died before they were six years old. In most cases the cause of death was officially unknown, for doctors were too expensive either to diagnose disease or to prescribe remedy. But there is no real doubt what killed them. The people of Haworth died because of the way they lived.

Within Haworth village there were 316 houses. Twelve had privies of their own, the other 304 shared fifty-seven between them. When the privies were drained at all, the excrement flowed along a shallow gutter into an open sewer that ran the length of Haworth's main street. Fifty midden-steads and twenty-three dung heaps stood amongst the houses. One heap was augmented by rotting entrails and the refuse from a nearby knackers yard. Eleven pumps supplied the village with drinking water. Occasionally they would break down. Often they would run dry. Invariably they were contaminated. Villagers in search of purer water walked half a mile up the hill past Haworth village. There the spring was foul, but fouled by beast rather than by man. To the more fastidious villagers that was some consolation.

The intelligentsia in and about Haworth must have known that the festering dung heaps and the fetid pumps killed the people who lived amongst them. Thirty miles away in Leeds, the Poor Law Medical Officer had investigated the connection between cholera and decent sanitation. Dr Baker's *Cholera Plan of Leeds* showed that the disease raged most fiercely and struck most frequently near stagnant becks and open sewers. Yet for eighteen years after the Great Cholera Epidemic (always ennobled in Civic Records by capital letters as if it was a victory in a colonial war or a visit by Queen Victoria) Leeds, in sight of the Pennine grit which produces the purest water in England, did nothing, and the 340 people who occupied thirty-four houses in Boot and Shoe Yard continued to share three earth closets.

Inevitably, a second cholera outbreak came. It swept across all of south Yorkshire in 1850. Two years earlier, whilst revolution was raging like a gale through continental Europe, a clean wind had begun to blow through the Yorkshire slums. It came too late to save the dead of 1850, but Edwin Chadwick's careful lists of death and disease had established a connection between sickness and sanitation certain enough to ensure the passing of the great Public Health Act of 1848. The pressure from Parliament combined, two years later, with the deaths on their own doorsteps, convinced the burghers of Leeds that their city needed "an ample supply of the pure beverage of nature". By 1856 the work was finished and water from the Wharfe flowed into Eccup reservoir and from there into the town.

Huddersfield, Halifax and Hull enjoyed a public water supply long before Chadwick's Act focused the nation's attention on urban disease and urban death. But all over the county there was passionate resistance to the "interference with personal liberty" that the Act encouraged and the expense that implementing the Act involved. At Harrogate, rate-payers insisted that worthy citizens had wells in their own gardens and that a general supply of clean pure water would only benefit the un-deserving poor. At Hull, the local Health Board surveyor confessed that he only survived because of the "protecting clauses" of the Act which allowed him to ignore the illegalities of local vested interest. George Hudson insisted that, at least in York, conditions were not as bad as Chadwick claimed.

There is no doubt how they were in Sheffield. The 1848 *Report on the Sanitary Conditions in the Borough of Sheffield* describes it as "one of the most unhealthy towns in the Kingdom". In the Wicker a single privy was used by nineteen families and a nearby school of sixty children. In Sylvester Lane there was "scarcely a yard of ground ... not covered by filthy water from houses and privies". Again there was a shortage of good clean water. Sheffield, now surrounded by the reservoirs of Bradfield and Ladybower, then found "great difficulty in procuring a sufficient quantity for ordinary domestic purposes, much less for scouring their

"Church Triumphant"

"Work and Worship"

"Skylark's Song"

"Get Stuck In!"

"Before the Fall"

"Hard and Proud"

"Likely Lad"

"The Infant Gentleman"

"No Mean City"

"Glad Tidings to Zion"

"Builded
Here"

houses and courts when required". Life expectancy was thirty-two years and six months.

Keighley in 1848 was much the same. The owners of dwelling houses in Nelson and King Streets were summoned because "the privies—used in common by all the occupants of the houses in the said streets—are in such a filthy and unwholesome condition". Six years later the Inspector General of the Board of Health found sixty-nine houses that shared three privies and thirty houses that had no privies at all.

Chadwick's Act—although it lapsed in 1854 and was replaced by something much more to the liking of the thrifty ratepayers—must have saved a million lives in mid-century Yorkshire. Clean water began to flow right across the country. Closed sewers were buried underground along a hundred main streets and through a thousand yards. Gradually fewer and fewer Yorkshire families died because of the way they lived. But it was another fifty years before anyone took seriously the simple fact that thousands of Yorkshiremen died because of the way they worked.

In Sheffield, dry grinding in closed rooms filled the air and choked the lungs with particles of metal from the half-made knives and grit from the turning wheel. For 42s. it was possible to purchase a "Waddington Fan" which would blow at least some of the dust out of the "little mester's" window. But that was too expensive for most grinders to afford so they developed grinders' asthma and achieved an almost unique mortality rate. Six out of every ten died before they were thirty. Three of the survivors never saw their fortieth birthday. The long-lived tenth was dead before his fiftieth.

Men tunnelling to run the railways through the Pennines had a different future to which they could look forward. Some died from pneumonia, the result of days spent in wet clothes chopping their way through wet rock. A few were killed or maimed during drunken brawls, the direct product of a life so wretched that only gin could render it temporarily tolerable. Many more died or were disabled by falling rock and flying stone. Edwin Chadwick saw the Woodhead Tunnel that took the railway from Sheffield to Manchester as a battlefield. "The losses in this one work may be stated as three per cent killed and fourteen per cent wounded. The deaths in the four battles Talavera, Salamanca, Vittoria and Waterloo were only 2·11 per cent of privates." Woodhead does not stand alone on the battle honours. The Bramhope Tunnel on the Leeds to Thirk line cost the lives of twenty-three men. Their memory is kept green by a folly in Otley Churchyard, part tunnel, part castle. It is gradually crumbling away because it was built of cheap Caen stone.

IGY

At Haworth, wool combers, working in their own houses, kept high-temperature stoves burning day and night. The cottage windows were always tightly shut, keeping the air warm and damp and making the tangled wool easy to straighten and unravel. The men, women and children who breathed the hot damp air died of tuberculosis. They were taken to the churchyard at the top of the hill and committed to eternal rest and the hope of salvation by the Reverend Patrick Brontë.

To the east in Barnsley, Wakefield, Pontefract and Castleford miners were dying of the "dust". And those whose lungs survived or withstood air more composed of coal than oxygen expected at least one injury during their hacking and shovelling life from rock-fall or explosion. In and about Barnsley the most moving and marvellous pieces of stone are mementos mori.

On Kendray Hill a monument recalls the disaster of 1886. Three hundred and sixty-one men died. Some were killed at the instant of the great explosion. Others, less fortunate, were carried home to die of their burns, for there was no hospital within twenty miles. The day after the first awful flash of fire, a single survivor rang the rescue bell. He was hauled out half alive and a party of volunteers was lowered down the shaft to see if anyone else was left to save. They had been underground five minutes when a second explosion engulfed them all.

In Silkstone churchyard a modest memorial points a moral from the flood of 1838.

This monument was erected to perpetuate the remembrance
of an awful visitation of the Almighty which took
place in this parish on the 4th Day of July 1838.
On that eventful day, the Lord sent forth His Thunder,
Lightning, Hail and Rain carrying devastation
before them and by a sudden eruption of water
into the Coalpit of P. C. Clark Esq, twenty-six human
beings whose names are recorded here were suddenly
summoned to appear before their Maker.
READER REMEMBER
Every neglected call of God will appear against thee
on the Day of Judgement. Let this solemn warning
sink deep into thy heart and prepare thee so
the Lord when He comes may find thee
WATCHING

It seems unlikely that the twenty-six miners of Silkstone had consciously prepared themselves to stand before the glory seat. No doubt, if they thought about it at all, they thought they could begin their WATCHING in a year or two. Amongst them was "George Birkinshaw, aged ten years" and "Joseph Birkinshaw, aged seven years, his brother". They share a grave with "Sarah Newton, aged eight years" and "Elizabeth Clarkson, aged eleven years" (she lies at the feet of her brother, James Clarkson). When P. C. Clark Esq. meets in heaven his employees who died that day, he will discover that the youngest was five and the oldest fourteen.

By the time I got to Barnsley, Old Oaks and Silkstone had passed into folk-lore. They are part of ancient history like the Wednesday Fair granted by Henry III in 1249. But on Wednesdays, Barnsley still buys cut-price shirts and only slightly damaged crockery from stalls in its open market. The old days have not completely passed. The homes of the great and gracious have become teachers' training colleges. Open-cast mining has come and gone. The post-war Poles who reinforced the colliers' army have been successively rejected, accepted and forgotten. But backs are still broken and lungs are still destroyed in the last of the horrific and heroic occupations that made "hard" and "proud" the qualities we naturally associate with Yorkshire.

The adjectives end a thousand Yorkshire stories. As the desolate church wardens turn their pregnant daughters into the snow, as bankrupt mill-owners refuse to compromise with starving workers, as dying consumptives forbid their estranged brothers to pay the doctors' bills, as the collier cuckold rescues his wife's lover from the flooded pit but refuses to shake his hand, the play can only end with a single line—"You're a hard, proud man. Hard and proud." If you want to know how and why the story began, go to Barnsley.

THE INFANT GENTLEMAN

MIDDLESBROUGH IS A frontier town, divided from Durham by only sixty yards of cold grey Tees, and true to the traditions of the frontier, it was built in a hurry. In 1800 there were twenty-five people in Middlesbrough village. By 1860, nineteen thousand souls lived and worked on the five hundred acres of land which made up the Middlesbrough Estate Limited. By 1900, there was a town of ninety thousand citizens, complete with new Town Hall, Cathedral and Stock Exchange. In fact, Middlesbrough became the Klondike of Yorkshire, the product of the great coal and iron rush. It is a town with hardly any past, anxieties about its future and uncertainties even about the reality of the present.

According to Mr Gladstone, Middlesbrough was "the youngest child of England's enterprize . . . an infant gentleman but . . . an infant Hercules". The modern traveller can only conclude that it outstripped its strength, grew too quickly to grow well and developed a strain of urban rickets that has yet to be properly treated and fully cured. There can be no town in England with more dereliction within a mile of its Town Hall. To the casual visitor it seems that most of Middlesbrough is boarded up, knocked down or just left to crumble away.

Much of the town centre is temporary mud and cinder car park, designed in the style of bomb site circa 1955. Down by the world-renowned Transporter Bridge—a giant, horizontal funicular railway that carries cars and passengers across the river dangling at the end of a dozen steel hawsers—dereliction turns into desolation. On the eastern horizon, between the bridge and the sea, a Victorian clock tower still tells the right time. But the visitor arriving in Middlesbrough across the Tees from the north is greeted by a long façade of broken glass and missing slates. Single walls, the remains of what were factories, gape with black windows and frameless doors. To move on into the town, the motorist must cross a disused railway line. Modern Middlesbrough is the child of the railway age and the twisted rails are a tribute to the heavy industry that made the infant giant grow. But they are also a rusty reminder that the triumph of iron and coal left a lot of casualties in its victorious path.

In Middlesbrough, the demand for hardboard and plywood must be gigantic. It is nailed to window after window as if boarding up is a traditional feature of Middlesbrough life, part of Cleveland folklore that father urges son to observe and families follow as a mark of respect to the boarding up done by their forebears. Whole rows of shops are boarded up. Three-sided Edwardian bay windows are boarded up, a terrace at a time. In South Street, the Paris Restaurant (Proprietor, Hamed Saleh) is boarded up. Around the old Town Hall (having been successively turned into a police station, a markets office and a fire-engine garage, its tower is now a beacon which calls the old and the sick to St Hilda's clinic) new council maisonettes form a protective square. In three of the blocks—Mason House, Byers House and Chapman House— the windows of the ground-floor flats are boarded up.

Somehow the people of Middlesbrough seem to have triumphed over the ravages of time and the industrial revolution. They have risen above the privations of strike and depression. They have overcome the penalties of life in a town where, thanks to three distinct spasms of different industrial growth, there is more evidence of nineteenth-century industrial squalor than in any other town in Yorkshire. They have transcended the problems of living in a borough which changed its identity—Middlesbrough, Teesside, Cleveland—so quickly that the local council never had a chance to exploit the sixties boom in urban building and build a city its citizens deserved. They are not real Yorkshiremen and Yorkshirewomen. Some medieval boundary line put the land south of the Tees in the county, but the men who rushed to live and work in nineteenth-century Middlesbrough came not from the Three Ridings but from the four Kingdoms of Great Britain and Ireland. In 1871, only half of Middlesbrough's population had actually been born in Yorkshire.

The men who settled down to export coal, and their sons who made the steel and built the ships, came to call themselves "Yorkshire". But this is not what their descendants sound. They do not speak with the cautiously modulated broad vowels of their native county. Their sentences rise in pitch and tone at the end with Geordie near-hysteria. Middlesbrough is far less "tha what?" than "Howway man".

That makes Middlesbrough more kindly than careful, less hard than human. In the time it took to serve a single fillet of plaice, a Middles-brough waitress managed to display four distinct, but equally endearing, emotions and accompanied each show of friendly feeling with a playful, but painful, punch on the shoulder. There was approval of the acceptance of wine without the ritual tasting—"most of them that does it don't know why they do". There was disagreement with the decision not to eat chips—"don't worry about being fat, pet". There was disappointment at the refusal to accept a slice of lemon—"squeeze it on the fish, it takes the greasy taste away". And there was horror at the habit of holding the fork in the right hand—"my mother used to say it was like eating with a shovel".

No town in Yorkshire has inhabitants more willing to talk to strangers and less likely to be contemptuous of their local ignorance. Once, just outside Barnsley, I asked an apparent octogenarian the way to Upper Tankersley. His answer was clear but uncommunicative. "If tha don't know the way to Upper Tankersley, tha knows nowt." That is not how they treat travellers in Middlesbrough. There is a hundred-year tradition of new people moving in. South Yorkshiremen asking questions about the Town Hall and the Empire Theatre get civil answers.

The Empire—as its name implies—is reminiscent of a glory won far away from Middlesbrough. It is built of sandstone as red as the fort at Delhi, and has the rectangular solidarity and heavy towers of a garrison church, built at the zenith of the Raj. Now it is the home of Mecca Bingo, but its dependable dignity survives the day-glo posters.

Next door, the "new" Town Hall is classic Victorian gothic, a celebration of the renaissance and the reformation which were thought to have arrived simultaneously in nineteenth-century industrial England. It is decorated with little pink marble columns and boasts a huge rose window in one of its innumerable gables. It has enough doors for every member of the Council to enter in separate triumph and at the front a double entrance is approached by converging flights of marble stairs. They climb the outside wall and meet at the first floor—the sort of stairs that kept the Doge's feet dry when the water rose in Venice, and the Grand Canal flowed half way up the palace walls.

Middlesbrough was built on a hill, expressly to avoid such disasters. Alone amongst Yorkshire towns it was consciously created; done, as they say in the north, on purpose. In 1830 Joseph Peace extended the Stockton to Darlington railway line to what he called Port Darlington, a deepwater dock, from which south Durham coal could be exported to the world. Overlooking the new port was the hamlet of Middlesbrough, still standing on the high ground where St Cuthbert consecrated a chapel at the request of St Hilda of Whitby and with the intention of keeping it safe from the rising Tees. Peace bought five hundred acres of land that ran up and over Middleburg hill. The object of the purchase was wholly commercial, as the name of the venture—Middlesbrough Estate Limited—implies. Peace intended to house the colliers and dockers who came to work on the Port Darlington quay. But he intended to house them well. Wide, straight streets were cut into the open countryside. Land was allocated and space reserved for a town hall, a market, a bank and a chapel.

Of course, the good intention did not last. When the second wave of immigrants arrived at the Middlesbrough of the 1850s, there was no opportunity or inclination to pause and plan. Whole terraces of cheap houses were hurriedly built in the wide back gardens that ran between the rows of carefully designed villas. In 1851, there was no time to be lost. Iron ore had been found in the Cleveland hills. A new Middlesbrough was about to be built. This time it was to be made from iron and steel.

Henry Blacklaw and John Vaughan were, to the second new Middlesbrough of the industrial revolution, what Romulus and Remus were to Rome. The empire they created was industrial Teesside and their story is embedded in the history and archaeology of Cleveland. The houses in which they lived side by side still stand in Queen's Square. Henry Blacklaw was Middlesbrough's first Mayor and first Member of Parliament. He was the first Chairman of the Middlesbrough Chamber of Commerce and as Chairman of the Royal Middlesbrough Exchange he laid the foundation stone of the bourse they built on the bank of the Tees. The building survives at the heart of the town's history as a symbol of the great amalgamation of Middlesbrough iron and steel.

Dorman Longs—established in 1870 and amalgamated with Blacklaw and Vaughan in 1929—had for a head office a fine Victorian house with a classical portico over its front door and corinthian capitals on either side of its windows. The house cum office juts out from what was Henry Blacklaw's Royal Middlesbrough Exchange and faces across the street another great sign of Victorian civic virtue, the cast-iron public urinal. The entire building—the Dorman Long house at one end, the carved plaques of the Middlesbrough Exchange at the other—is still in the steel trade. Over its nineteenth-century portals a wholly twentieth-century legend has appeared: "British Steel Corporation, General Steel Division, Development Engineering Department, Teesside."

For most of the nineteenth century, Middlesbrough was an iron not a steel town. In the decade after iron was struck in Cleveland, annual ore production from that single field rose to half a million tons. Ten years later, in 1871, the north-east yielded up five and a half million tons and Teesside made two million tons of pig-iron (nearly a third of the total British output) in the single year. Sheffield, at the far south of the county, was using Henry Bessemer's invention to pour out molten steel soon after the end of the Crimean War. But Cleveland ore could not be used in his miraculous converter. So Middlesbrough stayed at the very heavy end of heavy industry.

It is still a heavy industry, but heavy industry is getting lighter. Now Middlesbrough makes steel, benefiting from the new techniques that began with the open hearth furnace. Competitors have contracted their production. Even in Middlesbrough the Cleveland Works are to close. But by 1980, Teesside should be making eleven million tons of steel each year, three times as much as in the early and middle seventies. It will not be made without the help of sweat. But it will be easy work compared with the days when Middlesbrough was the toughest town in Yorkshire, the place to which male workers emigrated leaving their wives and sweethearts safe at home. Today a man from Middlesbrough makes two hundred tons of steel a year. The Japanese steelworker—not thanks to bigger muscle or greater skill, but because of superior machinery— averages four times as much. The new South Teesside works is to emulate Japanese efficiency in the production of steel from iron-ore that comes into a new, specially designed dock at Cleveland. The wheel will have turned almost full circle.

In a way, Peace's hope will have come true. "Port Darlington" will be the great mineral dock of the north-east, but it will import iron-ore not export coal. Teesside will be the home of a new sophisticated steel industry, more advanced than Vaughan and Blacklaw could have dreamed, but benefiting from the skill of local labour and the example of foreign ingenuity. The long industrial war with Stockton is over and won. Middlesbrough, whose postal address was once "near Stockton", has become the undisputed champion of Teesside, and its Newport Bridge is in permanent repose to prove it. Once its two hundred and sixty-five foot span was hoisted in the air to allow the great ships to pass on their way up the river. Now the great ships never want to sail any further than Middlesbrough. So the red and white bridge lies rigid between its towers.

Middlesbrough may, after its innumerable incarnations, be finally coming into its own and joining modern, twentieth-century urban civilisation. It already has some of the less attractive marks of the new age—a huge metallic multi-storey hotel and a huge glass unoccupied multi-storey office block. There are still a lot of old houses to knock down and a new town centre to be built up. But there is the prospect of a native industry that keeps the town and its people permanently prosperous and takes the old brutality out of the way that Teesside earns its living. From now on there will be less certainty of sweat and less fear of the dole. The infant giant has grown up and is settling down.

NO MEAN CITY

ONCE UPON A time, Leeds City Square was the most famous—and most controversial—urban half-acre in all Yorkshire. It was dominated, rather improbably, by the Black Prince: a huge bronze warrior sitting astride a huge bronze horse and pointing menacingly towards the south and the enemy. But it was neither his slightly incongruous presence nor his highly belligerent pose which caused the anguish and the argument. It was the figures grouped around him that excited emotions and perhaps even aroused passions. For guarding the perimeter of the City Square were eight near-naked ladies.

They were, of course, allegorical figures. Four represented The Even: four The Morn. All eight were unambiguously feminine and undeniably undressed. Each epitomised that special combination of prurience and purity in which late Victorian artists specialised. In an attempt to dress up vice to look like civic virtue, each lady was given a torch to hold aloft. But they made improbable lamp-posts.

For years none of their obvious attributes seemed to matter. The eight identically firm bosoms and the eight identically rounded stomachs left the Victorians totally unmoved. The eight identical chignons and eight identical long noses must have reminded every passer-by of the illustrations in the *Strand Magazine* and the fashion plates in the *Ladies Home Journal*. But if nineteenth-century Leeds associated the statues with human female flesh it either did not care or kept its concern concealed. It was the middle classes of the late forties and early fifties—armed with the self-righteousness that comes from clothing coupons and utility furniture—who wrote angry letters to the *Yorkshire Post*. The eight naked ladies ought to be removed from public view. Their effect on the young and the impressionable could hardly be overstated.

I first saw them when I was fifteen. To put it more precisely, it was during my sixteenth year that the naked ladies of Leeds and I were first together in the same square. If I looked upon them, I recall it not. I was concerned with more serious business. Cricket had brought me to Leeds—the city in which the Yorkshire County Club had made its home and the ground on which Australia played its Yorkshire Test Match. The City Square was the site of the Queen's Hotel and the Queen's Hotel was the temporary home of the tourists. So I stood outside the front entrance of that extraordinary example of metroland-moved-north and waited to see the giants of 1948 drive off to Headingley.

Don Bradman looked exactly like the cigarette card. His jaw really was as square as the jaw in the picture, not as I feared photographically amputated to suit the shape of a packet of five or ten. Lindwall was there, so was Tallon and Miller and Hassett. So was Neil Harvey, only four years my senior but about to bat number six for Australia. He wore a yellow shirt and green tie with his purple suit. Sartorial envy exceeded sporting admiration. By half past five Harvey had scored a hundred—a "century on debut", the most romantic of all Test Match achievements. Later that night, I relived it stroke by stroke for my father. My awe at the innings was transmitted to him but my admiration for the suit proved less infectious. Purple, my father believed, ought only to be worn by ambulance drivers on duty.

Despite the eccentric taste in clothes that the trip revealed, my mother agreed that the excursion to Leeds had been a great success. For the next ten years I visited the city every other month. I sat in the Victorian pavilion at Headingley or stood on the terraces at the Old Elland Road. Once I even batted in Roundhay Park. But, by the end of that sporting decade, Leeds had come to occupy a new place in my heart and mind. Leeds worried me. Leeds was in constant competition with my native Sheffield. It was the other big Yorkshire city. It fluctuated from just below to just above our size. Industrially we both depended on steel and heavy engineering and lived in determined rivalry. Most menacing of all, Leeds Aldermen and Corporation seemed to offer a constant if covert challenge to our Aldermen and Corporation.

About some things we, in the Sheffield City Council Labour Group, harboured neither doubt nor uncertainty. We had a bigger majority than theirs and we had a thirty-year history of continuous Labour rule which they could not match. But Leeds had two manifestations of genuine civic virtue unrivalled throughout Yorkshire and beyond. They had Leeds Town Hall and Quarry Hill Flats.

In the late fifties Leeds "new" Infirmary (an obvious first cousin to St Pancras Station, designed by Gilbert Scott, but easily mistaken for Charles Barry's vision of Camelot) was unknown to me. I had never even heard of the superb oval Corn Exchange. My first visit there was a privilege denied until steel scaffolding criss-crossed under its dome like a three-dimensional spider's web and the offices which open off the wrought-iron balcony around the Exchange floor only advertised Brillo

Pads and cheap holidays in Tunisia. But almost twenty years before I
saw Cuthbert Broderick's parabolic masterpiece—whilst wheat still
covered its sampling tables, its auctioneer's rostrum still felt the hammer,
and cheques were still written and banknotes still counted in its Settling
Room—I knew about the Town Hall the same architect designed. I
believed it to be a mark of unique nineteenth-century municipal distinction. Quarry Hill Flats seemed an equal testimony of what a modern city
could achieve.

The Town Hall in Leeds—unlike its Sheffield namesake—was not the
place in which the Corporation did its daily business. It was designed as a
home for oratory and oratorio, but its real purpose was the celebration of
the power and prestige of Queen Victoria's municipal empire. But symbols
of power and prestige cost money, and Leeds, after all, is Yorkshire. So
the passion to build a hall commensurate with civic dignity was matched
by a determination that it should cost not a penny more than dignity
required. Quality competed with economy. The desire for class vied with
the obligation to be careful.

The desire for quality was most sharply felt by the hopeful middle
classes, the people who knew that they lived in an age of improvement
and felt moved to perpetuate the standards of their time in stone. They
carried the day at a meeting called "to ascertain the feelings of the inhabitants as to the erection of a large public hall". But the people of Leeds
proved more willing to cast their votes than invest their savings. The
ten-pound shares, intended to finance the great adventure, found few
buyers and the proponents of the scheme were thrown back on the last
refuge of impecunious philanthropists—if the thing was worth doing, it
was worth doing out of the rates.

A resolution proposing, in effect, that since the city would not behave
responsibly towards the Town Hall, the Town Hall should become a
civic responsibility was tabled during October 1850. It was carried
in January 1851 by 24 votes to 12, after the November elections had
given the enfranchised citizens of Leeds the theoretical right to vote
for candidates who wanted neither the rates nor the Town Hall
to go up. But the battle was not over. Indeed it had barely begun.

To ensure that concept, design and execution were equal in their
perfection, the City Fathers called up the architectual heroes of the day.
Joseph Paxton—his Crystal Palace still shining and new—was consulted.
Sir Charles Barry—his Houses of Parliament not yet complete—adjudi-
cated in the competition to decide which privileged architect would
actually put pencil to paper. He chose Cuthbert Broderick of Hull, and

mentioned in passing that dignity could only properly be served if the design incorporated a suitable tower.

Suitably dignified towers are expensive. The one for Leeds Town Hall was estimated to rise to a height of £6,000. That, the Council decided, was too far. The argument raged on for five more years. In 1854 a resolution to set aside £7,000 for the addition of a tower was defeated by seven votes. In 1856 a scheme to produce a cut-price version for £5,500 was approved. But all that was only a skirmish in the war between architectural quality and financial caution. Broderick and the builder were in continual conflict, the builder demanding more money and the architect insisting on a bigger labour force, better workmanship and earlier completion.

Sometimes economy triumphed and brave new ideas were abandoned altogether. The scheme to fill the auditorium with paintings by eminent Victorians simply failed through lack of funds. Sometimes caution prevailed and Broderick was forced to accept the dangerously lowest tender. One Mr Noble received the contract to sculpture the eight lions which guard the Town Hall steps because he was prepared to breathe feline life into inanimate stone for £600—and offered for no extra charge to visit Regent's Park Zoo to see what lions really looked like.

Those lions still stand guard. Wind and weather have brought on a bad attack of the mange. Their manes are no longer precisely defined, their claws are blunted, their muzzles worn down to Pekinese proportions. But the Town Hall itself is intact. Despite all the efforts at economy, it turned out to be a good solid Yorkshire job with a final cost of £122,000—£80,000 or 60 per cent more than was originally intended. That was the result of Cuthbert Broderick's proper Yorkshire obsession with quality, his rejection of stone which he feared would crumble and the destruction he wrought with his own hand and hammer of coping stones and cornices which he knew would not last.

Monuments are often built with that high quality and care, and Leeds Town Hall is essentially a monument to the City Fathers of the time, built by them as a memorial to themselves and their values. Quarry Hill Flats were built, a hundred years later, with no better object than providing houses for the poor. So in their construction the obligations to quality were ignored. The responsibility lies neither with the visionary who conceived them nor the architect who designed them. Perhaps the builder—Tarrant of Hull, the self-made millionaire from Cuthbert Broderick's city—was caught between the cost of raw materials and the price the Corporation could afford. But whatever the reason, twenty-five years after the first tenants moved in, it cost two and a half million pounds to keep Quarry Hill upright, weathertight and safe. Ten years later, the struggle to keep them habitable was finally abandoned and the argument began about what should replace them—new flats, an urban park or the sort of offices which yield high rates.

None of which should diminish the achievement which Quarry Hill represents. When the patron saint of City Councillors enters the names of worthy cities in his golden book, Leeds will qualify not because of the Town Hall, but on account of Quarry Hill. The first was the product of pride. The second was born out of compassion.

Quarry Hill Flats were an unlikely addition to the Yorkshire of the 1930s. Their true begetter was Charles Jenkinson, parish priest and Leader of the Labour Group on Leeds City Council, whose squeaky cockney voice and rusty bicycle became part of Yorkshire folk-lore. Jenkinson said and did things about municipal housing which had never been said and done before. He concocted the notion that the poor should pay less for their houses than the well-to-do and thus invented the principle of "differential rents". He visited Vienna where the "workers' flats" had been produced in a quantity and at a speed which he had hitherto believed to be impossible. He saw Karl Marx House "with a frontage of about half a mile by 120 yards wide—that is to say nearly the whole length of Kirkstall Road from West Street to the Viaduct". Stifling both his prejudices against the manifestations of communism and his natural preference for traditional two-storey semi-detached workers' cottages, he decided to build something big in Leeds. And he determined something more than that. He insisted that the industrial poor, decanted from the city's grimmest slums, should have a safe and sanitary method for the removal of their rubbish and their refuse. It would be piped out of their kitchens, carried away in a continuous flow of good Yorkshire water.

Twenty years after Quarry Hill was completed, putting aside our prejudices and our pride, we went from Sheffield to learn from Leeds. The new, and much better, flats we built are a tribute to Jenkinson even if no one in South Yorkshire would ever admit it. They will remain in praise of him long after Quarry Hill is pulled down.

Then Leeds will have only two distinctive landmarks—the Town Hall and the Stephenson Building of the University—which travellers will see and instantly recognise as they drive west into the city from Lancashire across the Pennine motorway, or leave to the south and watch the hall-marks disappear over their left shoulders. The city cannot be quite the same without Quarry Hill but it will survive its passing as it has survived other changes.

The City Square no longer excites interest or admiration. The Black Prince, once its dominant splendour, is now overshadowed by the giant lights erected to illuminate him and dwarfed by the terrazzo and glass offices that hem in the square. The Australian cricketers have abandoned the Queen's Hotel. Even the near-naked ladies have moved. In front of the black Post Office stand statues of the great, the good and the once (locally) respected. The Morns and the Evens have been relegated to one side of the triangle which is now the City Square. They face each other in double file like a self-conscious guard of honour at a nudist wedding.

No doubt they think of better days—days before they filled the correspondence columns of the *Yorkshire Post*, an age of Edwardian serenity when aristocratic abandon was accepted and washing away the refuse of the poor was unthinkable. With their chignons, their aquiline features and their brazen ways they are not the sort of ladies who lived in Quarry Hill Flats. But they ought to be proud to stand in the city which built them.

LIKELY LAD

W HEN I WAS twelve I was desperate for the ownership of the steel industry to pass into different hands—mine. I was not moved by the national interest, filled by a desire to stimulate production or fired by a determination to increase investment. I just wanted to own some of those tall black chimneys and deep golden furnaces.

I compiled an envious list of the great names of Sheffield steel—Osborne, Doncaster, Vickers, Steel, Firth, Tyzack, Tozer and Peach. I knew the gaunt grey houses they had built in the smoke-free south-western suburbs. I could recite lists of their overlapping directorships and remember whose grandfather played baccarat with Edward VII at Tranby Croft. During the annual taxi ride which completed my summer visit to Bridlington, or Mablethorpe, I travelled home from the station with my nose pressed hard against the window, fascinated by the billets and blooms in the stockyard below the station approach and hypnotised by the red glow that hung over the Wicker and Shalesmoor. I was in thrall to the steel-masters, to their steel and to the huge corrugated iron sheds in which they broke and bent it.

When I am old I shall certainly pretend that at twenty-one the finger of fate beckoned me home to Sheffield and that, replete with a new and shiny BSc(Econ), I determined to become, if not a captain of my native industry, at least a corporal. It will be an old man's fantasy. I returned to home and steel simply because I was not sure where else to go. My love affair with stamping and forging had been eroded by youthful cynicism and overlaid by an all-consuming passion for politics. Throughout my finals' year I had toyed with the nation's great manufacturing companies, hoping—irrationally and vainly—that an academic miracle would free me from industry altogether. The miracle mirage faded, both ICI and the Ford Motor Company lost patience with my hesitance to deliver myself into their hands, and five weeks before finals and seven before my wedding day I was still potentially unemployed.

It was then that the "makers of high quality steel pressings, forging extrusions and drop stamping: established 1781" came into my life. It was not a large or fashionable firm, but it was available. I offered my services. Undeterred by the unfavourable omen of appearing for interview at the Efficiency Department on the wrong day, I gave the Managing Director a short lecture on mobile lifting gear (having seen an advertising film the day before in between *Movietone News* and *From Here to Eternity*), and waited for him to be impressed. Twenty years on, I can only assume that the lecture was forgiven and the confusion of dates overlooked. Incredibly, I was offered the job and I began to re-create the relationship that steel and I had once enjoyed. Having returned from the Trojan War, I found my old love still waiting and weaving her endless tapestry of crankshafts, propeller blades, car valves and steel balls.

George Orwell had written about Sheffield and steel in 1930. "Even Wigan is beautiful as compared with Sheffield. . . . If at a rare moment you stop smelling sulphur, it is because you have begun to smell gas. Even the shallow river that runs through the town is usually bright yellow with some chemical or other. Once I halted in the street and counted the factory chimneys I could see; there were thirty-three of them, but there would have been far more if the air had not been obscured with smoke." I knew the river and I recognised the chimneys, but I did not see Sheffield and its industry as Orwell described it. A hundred years before Orwell visited south Yorkshire, Cobbett rode across the West Riding, saw the native industries as I saw them and rightly judged that "nothing can be conceived more grand or more terrible than the yellow waves of fire that incessantly issue from the tops of the furnaces '.

In fact, my company was hardly characteristic of the South Yorkshire steel industry. For one thing, it was small, too small to be nationalised and too small to boast the sort of rolling mill which sends snakes of red-hot steel running backward and forward across the factory floor as it beats them thin and pulls them long. For another, it was still firmly under the control of the founding families. In fact it had virtually nothing in common with Steel, Peach and Tozers whose chimneys ran most of the way along the road that linked Sheffield to Rotherham; chimneys which when in full black spate had been photographed and immortalised in a picture postcard under the title of "Salubrious Sheffield". Nor was my company a near-monopoly like the Tinsley Wire Works whose product ran along fences in every country in the world. It did not have the association with heavy engineering which Vickers and Firth Brown enjoyed or the encouragement to innovate and modernise which went with it.

But, like its neighbours—for in Sheffield in the fifties there was no exception to the rule—it existed more as the product of history than the result of immediate economic forces. For nothing it needed, apart from skill, originated in Sheffield. It heated its furnaces by gas from Barnsley coal. And since in all south Yorkshire only one factory—Parkgate at Rotherham—actually *makes* steel, the great ingots that it hammered into three-foot steel rings were imported from north-east England and the south of Wales. That is what it did and that is what I found, instantly, if only initially, enchanting. It was, in fact, a big partly-mechanised blacksmith's shop. After sixteen years of unremitting education, I was to work for a blacksmith—like my grandfather did before he became a collier and a Communist and like Henry Hall did before he left Sheffield to become Welterweight Champion of Great Britain. I fell in love with steel again.

Sometimes it was easy to re-live all the old emotions. At six o'clock in the morning it was the most romantic place in the world. The furnaces glowed a friendly red instead of the fearful white that they glared later in the day. The hammer drivers all spent the first few minutes of the early shift striking speculative blows to test eye and find range. There was so much rolling of sleeves and flexing of muscles that it was possible to forget the holes in the tin roof and the oil in the sanded floor and believe that every day brought another twenty-four hours of victory in the battle which was industry in Queen Victoria's England.

That was in the early morning. For the rest of the day it was simple purgatory. For one thing, nobody really believed in graduates. There was a grudging acknowledgement of their existence, but an outright rejection of the notion that they might be helpful. Graduates were a concession to modernity and no one was going to waste time or money pretending anything else. In the early fifties some firms wasted the talents of their graduate trainees by flinging them into management innocent of any experience of how their industry worked, believing that they had nothing more to learn. I was taught nothing, not because I already knew enough, but because I was adjudged industrially ineducable.

There were, however, occasional periods of character-building—usually painful lessons in humility. One morning an Oxford historian and I poked about in the blocked-up drain with a piece of ineffectual wire. That at least broke the monotony. Most of the time I stood about watching other people work. Occasionally I held a stopwatch in my hand as part of an elaborate but ill-fated campaign to convince the workers that piecework rates were based on a more rational calculation than a shrewd guess at how little the management could get away with.

For long periods I did literally nothing. I arrived each morning a little late but appreciably earlier than other employees of my grade. The day began with tea made by an ex-submariner who, splendid in flat cap and

KGY

long brown dustcoat, then went off to fulfil his duties as heir apparent
to the manager of the saw shop. I then read the previous day's *Express*
and awaited instructions.

Sometimes they never came. Sometimes I did simple calculations with
all the complicated precision of a totally unnecessary slide rule. Sometimes I looked at stock cards and sales records seeking to understand them
in order that they might be improved. If they are better now than they
were twenty years ago, it is no credit to me. The secrets of only a few
were vouchsafed to me. The occasional improvements that I recommended were invariably turned down. Often I just talked to the "lads",
elderly employees past hope and retirement, who shuffled about sweeping
floors and making tea if there were no graduate trainees about to do it.
We shared the despair that comes of inactivity. The fearful prospect of
becoming a "lad" myself seemed at times to stare me in the face.

But it was not the sheer indestructible hopelessness of it all that finished
me. I could stand the refusal to employ engineers because of their tedious
tendency to agitate about new machinery and I could survive in offices
kept down to a dingy overcrowded minimum to ensure that executives
"got out into the works". I could even reconcile myself to the depressing
discovery that the names of the directors of this family firm were
exactly duplicated amongst my contemporaries and competitors.
It was the uncongeniality which was beyond endurance. I spent my life
with people who really believed that art galleries hung Picasso upside
down and no one knew the difference, who really did suspect that poets
were homosexuals, and who were certain that politics "is a dirty business"
and "knew" that the trade unions were acting on behalf of a foreign
power with the sole objective of destroying Western civilisation.

Officials of the Union of General and Municipal Workers whom I had
known since childhood—and suspected since those early days of unwill-
ingness to kill a wasp unless it stung them twice and only then after they
had tried to talk it into promising that it would mend its ways—were
described as Bolsheviks and worse. If Alderman Harold Slack had visited
the factory wearing a long cloak and concealing beneath it a black,
round, metal object labelled "bomb", they would not have been remotely
surprised.

They feared the closed shop more than they feared death and they
knew what Sheffield trade unionists do to obtain it. To begin with,
they remove essential components from the machines of honest working
men who have refused to join a union—a well-known practice called
"rattening". Then they drop gun-powder down factory chimneys,

blowing out gable ends and bankrupting "little mesters" who are not insured against such outrages. Employers who stand out against their tyranny receive ominous notes signed with sinister pseudonyms like "Mary Ann" and informers are shot at on dark nights when leaving public houses. None of that had, in fact, happened in Sheffield since 1866. But to my colleagues the memory of the "stirrings" was still fresh and green.

Robert Applegarth, being evidence for the defence, had been forgotten. I had always thought of him as bearing a remarkable resemblance to the Aldermen of the General and Municipal Workers Union. He founded the Sheffield Co-operative Society. He persuaded his branch of the Union of Carpenters and Joiners to move their monthly meeting from a public house to a reading room. And when he became one of the most powerful trade union leaders in the land, he told the Royal Commission,

> I set out from the first day I took office with the determination that I would not have anything to do with the violation of the law, and if there was any violation of the law in connection with our Society, I would bottom it.

Violations of the law come in all shapes and sizes. During my steel-making days, the biggest and worst was the invasion of Suez. Moralists who usually confined their wisdom to the proposition that all decent men and women are at home by half past ten, found a new scope for their virtuous advice. It was also an occasion for the exercise of judgement. As ex-soldiers they knew that the Israelis (whom they suspected of wearing suede shoes with crepe soles) would be overrun by the Arabs. (They talked much of Bedouin courage and Colonel Lawrence; an officer of whose idiosyncrasies they had not heard.)

But relief was at hand. One morning as I read *Brideshead Revisited* (carefully protecting it from the bacon grease which ran out of the mid-morning sandwich I was eating) a phone call told me of a job in adult education. I lost almost a hundred pounds a year but gained, for almost the first time, the approval of the management. "You have made," they assured me, "a wise choice." I left with no regrets and little experience, but two things were stamped in my heart and mind deeper than the company's trade-mark. The first was the absolute certainty that something had to be done about the steel industry. The second was the imperishable conviction that as far as I was personally concerned the steel masters could keep it.

KGY*

SEVEN

Builded Here

———————

BUILDED HERE

I WAS BORN and bred in a separate and special part of Yorkshire. Throughout my boyhood, I believed that further north was the Yorkshire of lore and legend, the world of whippets, the cow-heel country. But we in Sheffield were a more southern sort of tyke. Our Dukes were Derbyshire and their country houses tempted us to spend our summer Sunday afternoons beyond the county border. We shared our local regiment with Lancashire and where the city boundary ended, the Midlands began. Our rivers flowed south into the Trent, not east to join the Ouse. We were famous because of cutlery, a trade and a tradition so exclusive that its excellence isolated us from the history of the county as a whole.

Yet we felt a certain and secure part of Yorkshire, doubly blessed as a distinct part of the distinctive county. I assumed that the real Yorkshire was a combination of Bruddersford and Pudsey, a place where the accents were as broad as the acres, the woollen mills reverberated with the clatter of clogs and the blare of brass bands, and where one baby boy in five sprang into the world fully armed with bat and pads ready to play cricket for Yorkshire and England. But I felt neither envious nor superior about what I believed to be the life in the rest of the Three Ridings. I assumed that we were the border country, the barrier between our homogeneous brothers further north and the corruption of the south. Then I was allowed to venture out into the world beyond Sheffield and I began to realise that the rest of the county was too big to be all the same. I discovered Yorkshire to be a county of infinite variety bound together by virtues and values, but with countryside and customs that change from Riding to Riding, town to town, village to village.

My earlier excursions without either protective parents or anxious uncles were confined to the places where the Sheffield City Grammar School played cricket—the mining villages of the West Riding with modern municipal grammar schools of their own. Past Conisborough Castle and Manvers Main Colliery I batted against Wath and Mexborough. I fielded on Ecclesfields hill side and watched the Newton Chambers chimneys breathe black smoke and golden flames across the valley. On my way to play at Penistone, I walked in the awe-inspiring shadow of my first real Yorkshire viaduct, not a few arches spanning a river or road, but a celestial permanent way running right across the valley.

Those villages were not in the West Riding of my imagination, nor were they little replicas of the city they surrounded. They were a different sort of Yorkshire—places with diverse sights and sounds but common beliefs, similar principles and identical standards. When we played cricket the common beliefs and similar principles showed through the thin veneer of spurious sportsmanship. We all *needed* to win. Defeat was a disaster, personal failure was a disgrace. I struggled to be a good York-shireman glorying in the joy of combat and absolutely committed to victory—but I was always so worried about getting beaten.

If the purpose of playing cricket had been enjoyment and the result of each game incidental, I might have passed happy summer Saturdays. If we had played for pleasure, Friday evenings might have been spent in comfortable anticipation, oiling my bat and whitening my boots in preparation for the following day's festivities. As scoring twenty was a triumph which would sustain me until Sunday, but getting out for ten was a humiliation that stayed with me all week, Fridays were tense and Saturdays were terrible. I longed to get it all over, accomplish my little achievement and be freed from the duty to compete for a full seven days. Having made twenty was always a joy. But there was no joy in the making. That was a slow hour of desperate intensity, mind and muscle concentrated on the struggle to get behind the ball. I played forward to bowlers whose talents should have absolved them from wasting their time on me. I prayed that if I misjudged bounce, line or length the ball would hit my teeth rather than the edge of my bat. As I waited for the slips to appeal or the stumps to rattle, I learned my first Yorkshire lesson. There was nothing I could do except concentrate and carry on. Whatever I did, the ball would still be an indistinct red blur that only became visible when it was within six feet of my bat. The fielders would run me out whether I smiled at them or not. Despite my sunny nature and generous disposition, the wicket-keeper would catch me if he could. So although I could not grin, I learned to bear it.

I touched the peak of my cap between every ball in the way that Len Hutton touched his—not realising that even in England's opening bats-man it was a sign of nerves not professionalism. I choked on saliva generated by anxiety, and the gum I chewed to ape Keith Miller. In the nets, behind Spion Kop at Bramall Lane, I had been given the strictest instruction on how to respond when hit by a fast bowler. To show that it hurt would be both admission and encouragement so NEVER RUB IT!

That was easy. It was the pain that came from the ball missing me but hitting the wicket that was difficult to hide. But it was my Yorkshire duty not to let it show—to pretend that I felt confident, that I expected to prevail, that, if I was out without troubling the scorers, my dismissal was a denial of the laws of nature that could not be repeated next week. But as the bowler turned and began his long run-up, I always knew that he bowled for love and I batted for duty. Like Francis Norton I "longed to live at home in blameless ease". Like him I knew that the Standard of the North must be bravely borne. Like him I fell in battle (almost every Saturday afternoon) on a hillside in Yorkshire.

Years later in Hull, I visited a dockside public house kept by a man who never wore a collar with his flannel shirt, shaved only rarely and held up his greasy trousers with a war-surplus webbing belt. Behind his bar a dozen dirty velvet caps and three tarnished medals were half visible through the grimy glass of a plywood case. Hull was another different sort of Yorkshire, where little boys in Pearson Park played Rugby League. In his time, the landlord whose stomach hung over his khaki belt had been the finest professional wing three-quarter in the world. I was a few weeks away from finals and the apprehensions of the boy cricketer were being reproduced around my solar-plexus. I prayed that one day I too would feel that there was nothing left to prove, that the competition was over and the victory so complete that the caps and medals could be forgotten. But it was not the moment for idle day-dreams. I drank up and returned to my revision. The Yorkshire lesson had been learned. The obligation to succeed was absolute. Happiness had nothing to do with it. The call of competitive duty could not be denied.

Yorkshire was not to blame for my early obsession with results. Most of my formative years were devoted to the two human activities—games and examinations—which end at a stipulated moment with a formal verdict, failure or success, defeat or victory. And the late forties were combative times. The class to which I belonged was emerging and there was always the fear that the rest of my generation would move forward in perfect step leaving me solitary, conspicuous and unique in my immobility.

The obligation to compete was easier for me to accept than it was for some of my contemporaries. I was the only son of a regular *Guardian*-reading, occasional church-going, house-buying, Labour-supporting family. If, when Lord Butler wrote his great Education Act, he did not have me specifically in mind, then by coincidence, he exactly met my needs. Mine was the perfect eleven-plus family. I had been fashioned by fate and honed by environment to move inevitably (if not easily) from municipal grammar school to provincial university. But before the journey was quite complete, I had realised that for some people life's signposts were not quite so clear.

The second lesson came—of course in Yorkshire—during the 1950s. A. V. Alexander had been elevated to the peerage and I was a humble soldier in the army of George Darling, the new Labour Candidate for Hillsborough. As I canvassed a terraced house in Shalesmoor, the milk-man arrived. Yes, the lady would vote Labour. No, she could not pay the Co-op. Perhaps she was indolent, feckless and irresponsible. Perhaps she spent the housekeeping on Woodbines and brown ale, the furthest feckless irresponsibility could go in old Shalesmoor. But whatever the psychological cause or social reasons for her problems, I realised that I could not have done my homework in her kitchen. If life was a competi-tion, it was organised as an obstacle race and in Shalesmoor they had more hurdles and ditches than we had in Wadsley.

In fact, I was canvassing for a Party absolutely committed to the sort of social competition that came to be called "equality of opportunity". The eleven-plus was virtually invented in Sheffield by the Labour Councillors who had formed the City's government since before I was born. On two mornings every May, the so-called brightest and the supposed best were selected for a superior sort of education. The "scholarship" was designed to give the working class a chance. It was the scholarship that had sent me off in green cap and blazer to the Sheffield City Grammar School. The news had come after weeks of hope, days of apprehension and the utter despair of not receiving the long buff envelope by first post on the appointed day. When I got home from school, my father was in the front garden. "You've got five years at the City Grammar School."

The idea of giving boys and girls like me a "secondary education" could only have come to extra-ordinary men and could only have been made reality by extra-ordinary politicians. Time has altered the enlight-ened judgement about what equality really means. We know now that competition between the determined suburbs and the demoralised slums is hardly competition at all, and nothing to do with equality. But Ernest George Rowlinson did not know that. On the evening that followed Labour's sudden and unexpected victory, he was called from his engine driver's cab, to join Ernest Yorke (trade union official), Charles Gascoigne (gas fitter) and John Bingham (company secretary) running a city of five hundred thousand souls. They ran it according to the political arts and social sciences of the day and the socialist convictions of a lifetime.

When I arrived in the Sheffield City Council, Ernest George Rowlinson was a legend and a name engraved on the brass remembrance of past Lord Mayors. The Labour Group he had fashioned and formed was still in absolute control, able to increase the rates with the impunity only enjoyed by the truly invincible. We approached each May prematurely triumphant. If we lost every seat, the victories of other springs had ensured our majority until the end of the three-year cycle. We ran the City with fists of stainless steel, a metal no decent Sheffielder would cover with a velvet glove. We took all the Committee Chairmanships. We ensured that every board of school governors had a majority of Labour Party members. We met as a Labour Group on the Monday before the full Council Meeting and examined every sentence of the Council Minutes with meticulous care. By the end of the evening every line in the whole, hundred-page document was either official policy or subject to official amendment. There were no free votes. Any Councillor who sought, without approval, to alter philosophy, proposal or punctuation was automatically disciplined. When it was alleged that buffet teas encouraged absence from the Council floor, the whole principle of afternoon refreshment was debated by the Labour Group. By a narrow majority the running buffet was abandoned and a formal "sit-down tea" put in its place. We were whipped to vote for a "sit-down tea" at five o'clock and against the Tory amendment that it should be held at half-past four.

And we got things done. On the May evenings in Crookesmoor as I toiled up and down the hills of my Ward, I could solicit votes with the proof of achievement as well as the promise of success. In the late sixties, from the cobblestones of Addy Street and Springfield Road I could see the new houses rising on Woodside, in Gleadless Valley and along Park Hill across the Don and the Sheaf and the Porter. The "shallow rivers that ran through the town" were still "bright yellow with some chemical or other" as they were when George Orwell saw them. But I neither "stopped smelling sulphur" nor "began to smell gas". The factory chimneys were no longer "obscured by smoke". We had made Sheffield air the cleanest air in industrial England. Henceforth there would be no more grime and dust, by order of the Mayor and Corporation. We had pulled down "the gaunt four-roomed houses, dark red, blackened by smoke" and replaced them by flats and houses that people actually wanted to live in. From the top of my hills, I could see Weston Park, Hillsborough Public Library and Walkley Swimming Baths. They were the mundane achievement of a whole half century of City Councillors. Had they been asked about the poetry of politics, Sheffield's Labour Councillors would have looked at the questioner as if he were daft and answered "tha' what?" They believed that politics was about actions not words. They preferred taking a single halting step forward to talking about running a swift and graceful mile. They wanted to build the New Jerusalem but they spent little time speculating about its absolute and complete achievement. They knew it could not happen tomorrow and they knew it would not happen at all unless they bent their backs and began to build it brick by brick. That was the third lesson I learned in Yorkshire.

All that is now twelve years and two hundred miles behind me. It is twelve years since I sat in slightly elevated splendour at the head of the great oval table in Committee Room One and presided over the Housing Committee under the unswerving varnished gaze of John Arthur Roebuck MP—"If the honest advocacy of innumerable measures intended for the welfare of the people at large . . . constitutes failure, then perish from the scrolls of immortality all the Howards and the Hampdens that glorify humanity." It is twelve years since I shovelled snow and then drove to work armed with spade and sack of sand to see me through the drifts and over the ice. Two hundred miles away, bus conductors still call their customers "luv", angling shops still advertise "live bait", redlit boys still haul the fiery serpents of steel, footballers are still unjustly accused of "neshing it", the chapels still flourish, the shoe shop that designed its own advertising slogans in peace and war ("no more leather until Hitler is tanned") still offers "men's working boots".

All that is now as much a part of my past as the first Sheffield memories—diphtheria and the hypodermic as big as a bicycle pump; the sweets provided by the doctor for "little boys who do not cry"; the weeping and the promise fulfilled as the pastilles (actually lozenge-shaped with pictures of fruit on the wrapping paper) went back into the pocket. It all actually happened—the uncles off on a cycling holiday to Cromer with khaki shirts and shorts bought from Milletts' Army Stores, and the big zinc bowl sunk in my own bit of garden to act as a fish pond, but never actually stocked with fish because my grandma thought captivity was cruel. But it was part of a different life in a different country.

Of course I still go back—back to Hillsborough, to Bramall Lane, to the Town Hall on Council day, to Wadsley and to home. But although Sheffield is still part of me, I am no longer part of Sheffield. I am a visitor now; not an alien but an exile, half identified with the city that remains, half nostalgic for the city which used to be. But it is the place where I was formed and fashioned, where all the old emotions and attachments coincide. It is not the New Jerusalem but it is the place where first I saw the bow of burning gold.

Between the visits and the phone calls and the letters, it is Wednesday, December the 13th, 1972 that I remember most clearly. My father's death was not unexpected but everything about it was a surprise. Driving past the Town Hall, I could not believe that the great blue and green flag flew at half-mast for him. The pain was not the sort of pain I had anticipated. It was not sharp and sudden like a jumping tooth, but dull and heavy as if there had never been a time when the pain had not been there. It was a time of activity and organisation, a moment to welcome the catharsis that comes from preparation even though planning is no longer the same. The chapel organist, anxious to be helpful, pleaded with me to choose a different hymn as my choice could only result in embarrassment. The introduction was unrelated to the melody. A choral society might manage it—a congregation could not. Even after rehearsal it would be rough and ragged. Without practice it would be a fiasco. Was it the only hymn I wanted?

It was the only hymn I wanted. It was the only song I had ever heard my father sing from start to finish, the subject of the only musical anecdote he had ever told. Before I was sure who George V was (later, of course, I realised that he was the man who celebrated his Silver Jubilee during the year Sheffield Wednesday won the Cup) I knew he had told Hubert Parry that if the orchestra did not play *Jerusalem*, the King would whistle it himself. Of course the orchestra played. And so did the organist at the City Road Crematorium.

We arrived too early at the church, only a few seconds after Councillor John O'Keeffe and the battered Rover that he had driven all the way from Birmingham. At the back of the church was Gerald Broad—now an Inspector in the City Police but once a schoolboy batsman on Wadsley Common. At the front was Sir Ronald Ironmonger, leader of the South Yorkshire Metropolitan County Council but once Ron Ironmonger, Chief Whip, Chairman of the Water Committee and fanatical Sheffield Unitedite. The bearded curate—a card-holding member of the Manor Ward Labour Party—read from the Revelations of Saint John the Divine. "And I saw a new heaven and a new earth for the first heaven and the first earth had passed away. . . ." The organ played the introduction to the impossible hymn and we began in perfect time and impeccable unison. There was no need to read the words from the hymn-books. We had sung the hymn a thousand times before in other gatherings of the faithful. In moments of hope it was a prospect and a promise. At times of despair it was confirmation of conviction.

> I shall not sleep from mental strife
> Nor shall my sword sleep in my hand
> Till we have built Jerusalem
> In England's green and pleasant land.

INDEX

Compiled by Michael Slingsby Gordon

WESTMOR-

LANDIÆ

PARS.

DVNELMENSIS EPISCO: PATVS PARS

DARLINGTON

VRVM

Applegarth forest

THE WEST RIDI NG

KIRKBY LANSDALE

SETTLE

SKIPTON CAST.

Wharfdale

BRADFORTHE

Kainesburgh forest

RIPLEY

COLNE

HALYFAX

BARNESLEY

LANCASTRIÆ

PARS

CEST:

PARS

DERBIÆ PARS

STOPPVRTH